READING TO THE DEAD

A transitional grief therapy for the living

by

Barry J Peterson

Published by Audio Enlightenment Press.Com

Giving Voice to the Wisdom of the Ages

First Printing, 2014

1 2 3 4 5 6 7 8 9 10

ISBN 978-0-9910914-1-6

www.ReadingtotheDead.Com

www.AudioEnlightenmentPress.Com

A GNOSTIC AUDIO SELECTION

First "AudioEnlightenmentPress.Com" Printing

February 2014

TABLE OF CONTENTS

Authors Introduction

What if you lost a loved one, and were left emotionally and spiritually devastated? What if your loved one had never paid much attention, during life, to the spiritual side of existence? What if you had the ability to help in the spiritual realm, and at the same time help yourself move through the grieving process?

If you are one of the billions of souls who must, by sheer force of nature, experience conception, birth, life and death largely within the realm of the five earthly senses, you may view physical death simply as the end of life. Most people are so busy with their frenetic lifestyles that they are not even aware that there exists a life beyond the five senses, in a realm called the Supersensible World. Consideration of this expanded view takes us into the consciousness of the metaphysician or the theosophist -- a sphere rarely entered by the common person."

This book, though not an attempt to redefine the concept of death to the masses, is closely based upon the works of Rudolf Steiner, a German anthroposophist, philosopher and mystic, and on his own succinct views on life after death. His work is interesting enough to warrant a reconsideration of its own, not only as a stand-alone book, but also as a tool to help people going through a period of loss in their lives. Steiner's guidelines, gained through clairvoyant consciousness, can be approached as transitional grief therapy to help foster a more complete understanding of the death of a loved one, while assisting those left behind to come to terms with the separation. Valid options are available to aid in the spiritual evolution of the departed as well as our own process and continuation in the earthly realm.

If, like most enlightened thinkers following the commonly accepted belief systems of our time, you view death as a door or

1

transition from one vibrational state to another, this book will find a place of relevance in your life. If you are not ready to let go, or if you want to help contribute to the spiritual evolution of your loved one, then continue to read, and participate in your own evolution, as well. Once you start down this path, you will discover that you have within your reach not only the opportunity to help the soul of the departed, but also to help your own: "Verily I say unto you, Inasmuch as ye have done it unto one of the least of these my brethren, ye have done it unto me."

The fundamental, essential piece to this puzzle, the keystone to the wide arc of life, death and rebirth, is love. To take a very small excerpt from 1 Corinthians: "If I speak in the tongues of men or of angels, but do not have love, I am only a resounding a gong or a clanging cymbal. If I have the gift of prophecy and can fathom all mysteries and all knowledge, and if I have a faith that can move mountains, but do not have love, I am nothing. If I give all I possess to the poor and give over my body to hardship that I may boast, but do not have love, I gain nothing."

In fact, love is far more than this: it is the vibrational highway that connects you to a departed soul, the seed from which creation is sprouted and sustains itself. If you had no empathetic feelings, no love, and would choose to do this only out of filial duty, then save your time and resources, for such an effort will be to no avail. You may as well be trying to read sacred text to the wall or a dead oak tree in the back yard. The soul, whether the body is living or dead, is in a constant state of evolution. As the American mystic Neville Goddard so eloquently stated, "There is no limit to expansion or translucency, only contraction and opaqueness, which is humanity."

Before we decide how this works, it is necessary to delve a little more deeply into the anthroposophical realm, to understand why it works. This will impart clarity to your journey and give you a better understanding as to why your readings will be of benefit and will help to lift the departed soul higher, into a more receptive state.

This concept is hard for many people to understand, let alone believe, and it sometimes takes a little mental reinforcement from the established, orthodox view to give them the nudge they need to open their minds to accept new ideas. I can think of no better example of an established theology than that of the Catholic Church, to give a unique perspective on this topic, and I will take a few excerpts from Pope Benedict XVI's Encyclical Letter Spe Salvi to illustrate how subtly you must expand your consciousness in order to accept this theory. Pay particular attention to Paragraph 48, emphasis mine:

26. *It is not science that redeems man: man is redeemed by love.* This applies even in terms of this present world. When someone has the experience of a great love in his life, this is a moment of "redemption" which gives a new meaning to that life. But soon he will also realize that the love bestowed upon him cannot by itself resolve the question of his life. It is a love that remains fragile. It can be destroyed by death. The human being needs unconditional love.

48. A further point must be mentioned here, because it is important for the practice of Christian hope. *Early Jewish thought includes the idea that one can help the deceased in their intermediate state through prayer* (see for example 2 Macc 12:38-45; first century BC). The equivalent practice was readily adopted by Christians and is common to the Eastern and Western Churches.

The belief that love can reach into the afterlife, that reciprocal giving and receiving is possible, in which our affection for one another continues beyond the limits of death — this has been a fundamental conviction of Christianity throughout the ages and it remains a source of comfort today.

Who would not feel the need to convey to departed loved ones a sign of kindness, a gesture of gratitude or even a request for pardon?

And for that there is no need to convert earthly time into God's time: in the communion of souls simple terrestrial time is superseded. It is never too late to touch the heart of another, nor is it ever in vain. In this way we further clarify an important element of the Christian concept of hope. Our hope is always essentially also hope for others; only thus is it truly hope for us too.

As Christians we should never limit ourselves to asking: how can I save myself? We should also ask: what can I do so that others may be saved and so that for them, too, the star of hope may rise? When I ask that, then I will have done my utmost for my own personal salvation as well.

The death of a loved one is one of the most traumatic losses that any of us will have to experience in this lifetime. Teenagers often act as if death does not exist, while the elderly hang onto their lost dreams until the last breath is released, often regretting what could have been. Definite access to a method of help, for those who have never spent any amount of time contemplating the spiritual side of life, is at once comforting and logical in the evolutionary sense. To give people who are suffering through the loss of a loved one a way to help the departed and, at the same time, a method by which to ease their own internal pain, is of double benefit when both spiritual love and understanding are present. Even the unimaginable loss of a child can be eased once it is realized that the departed is an old soul, and that it is possible for us to help that soul reach the next step in the evolutionary process.

Understanding is the key to the grieving process, and with the gradual understanding of your role in a departed one's development, your loss, though still painful, will arrive at a much more tolerable state and duration. This has nothing to do with being a Christian, Catholic, Buddhist or Jew; this is an ancient, universal law that does not take into account religious difference or denomination. If there is love, there will be a connection. Do not take my word for it; you must prove it to yourself.

If there is a deep love between you and the departed, you will know that you are making a connection, and the feeling will come from the heart. With deeper understanding, you will begin to realize that spiritual love and connection are the key not only to life, but also to death and to the soul's journey into the next realms.

"External cultural life goes to its downfall. A time will come when the skies will be filled with airplanes; life on earth will wither, but the human soul will grow into the spiritual world."

"The earth is in a process of decay, and man participates very strongly in this process."

"True occult investigation does not shrink from reasonable criticism, but only from superficial criticism, which is no criticism."

Rudolf Steiner, Austrian philosopher, scientist and founder of the modern anthroposophical movement, produced during his lifetime a vast, singularly beautiful stream of knowledge addressing almost every aspect of human life and consciousness. The invention of Anthroposophy, shored up by a strong background in the theosophical movement of the late 19th century, allowed Steiner's rich and varied viewpoints with regard to the human spiritual condition to be brought forward in a form accessible to all.

All of his philosophical, psychic and scientific discoveries benefited humankind through their innate beauty, sensibility and logic. Steiner's work remains highly relevant; in fact, the reading of it may even have reached a high pitch of urgency today, given his prescient foreknowledge of modern environmental destruction, human materialism, educational deficiency and the massive threat to world agriculture and food supply presented by the loss of the honeybee.

Steiner gave selflessly to the anthroposophical community of his time, traveling by train for many years on a continuous lecture circuit throughout Europe. Between 1909 and 1923, he focused these talks largely upon the life of the soul between death and rebirth, as well on as the role of Christ and the Angels, or Higher Hierarchies, in the afterlife or spirit world. He provided explanations of extraordinary detail and clarity with regard to the deepest, most pressing questions of the human soul. Immediately preceding the latter decade and set of lectures, Steiner had carried out a two-year independent study on death and rebirth, journeying via clairvoyant consciousness to gather information in the spiritual realm.

His results have provided humankind with a highly specific outline of soul activity after physical death, along with vivid, living descriptions of the worlds beyond. In the pages that follow, all text supplied in quotes is referenced directly from Rudolf Steiner, as derived from his lectures:

Between Life and Death and Rebirth: The Active Connection Between the Living and the Dead, Lectures 1-16

Life Between Death and Rebirth in Relation to Cosmic Facts, Lectures 1-9

The Spiritual Hierarchies in the Physical World, Lectures 1-10

The Mission of Archangel Michael, Lectures 1-6

CHAPTER I

Life on Earth and Preparation for Passing through the Gate of Death

Our time spent living on earth in a physical body, and the choices we make while inhabiting this dense, privileged, often difficult realm, carry far greater spiritual import than we may realize while caught up in the rush and surface details of our everyday lives. Neatly caught between birth and death, this swathe of time during which we are allowed to live in a physical body represents our only chance to improve interpersonal relationships or to make amends to others. Creating peace and forgiveness with another becomes impossible after passing through the gate of death, when we must wait for a new physical life in order for the opportunity to present itself again. For souls having just experienced physical death, the ability to reach out to those with whom they were connected in the earthly realm -- and to other souls now inhabiting the spiritual world alongside them -- takes on immense emotional importance, thereby dictating the quality of their entire experience during the phase between incarnations.

During our time here on earth, we seek to cultivate an open, receptive outlook so that we may acquire essential spiritual knowledge and thereby pass through the portal of death in a state of peace and readiness for our further cosmic evolution. True kindness, morality and strong ethical and spiritual boundaries, especially with regard to the way we treat others, count for everything, and absolutely affect the life of the soul after physical death. During physical life, human beings commonly dwell in a state of unrest and upheaval because its clamoring demands action in direct opposition to the inner calm, restfulness and quietude necessary for a meditative state of mind. Paradoxically, earth is the only place where we have the chance to develop karmically and spiritually in the area of our relationships. After death, we acquire distinct faculties of spiritual cognition directly relevant to the advancement of the soul toward the next life, but nothing can be changed, healed or modified in the spiritual world that has been left incomplete in the earthly realm.

The experience of attaining knowledge in the spiritual world stands in direct contrast to the experience of attaining it in the physical plane, and is far removed from anything we could begin to imagine within the usual context of earthly life. Knowledge acquired here in the sensory world is vastly different from that processed in the spiritual world where, lacking the use of the five physical senses, we process all information purely through the spiritual self. Everything we have come to know is reversed, as if in a mirror image. In the physical world, we use our minds and bodies to move through our day, reaching out and shifting location; perception arrives almost exclusively through the senses, and is often taken for granted as we proceed, sometimes distractedly, through the course of our days. In the spiritual world, the situation is reversed. There, the more still we can remain and the less we struggle to acquire, the more inner silence we are able to cultivate — the greater the knowledge we are able to absorb through visions, our only means of perception in the heavenly realm. Our spiritual sight becomes the only means by which we may communicate and learn. In both worlds, however, no matter which side of the veil we find ourselves inhabiting, inner calm draws to us a greater number of souls who may be of help."

Humans living on earth are, often unwittingly, intimately connected with universal life and the greater cosmos. The intense synchronicities we acknowledge with gasps of wonder between friends, but more often dismiss as mere coincidence in the societal push to retain a solely linear, scientific, conformist view of the physical realm, are completely real. Just as humans on earth are capable, under favorable circumstances, of communication with the dead, souls from the other side are capable of communication with us -- as are the angels, called the Higher Hierarchies in Anthroposophy. These magnificent, peaceful, powerful beings can influence the course of events in our lives through their own spiritual kindness and brilliance, sometimes saving us from accident or distress by intervening at just the right moment. They may cause us to be late, for example, when we thought we had to be on time, only to find out later that the train, plane or route we would have taken had run into severe complication or danger. They may create openings in our lives where we once could see only obstacles, because with their overarching vision, they can see the best route for us to take, the most favorable avenue we can pursue at any particular moment.

Ordinary souls, who have already passed to the next world, also possess the capability of protecting those still living in the physical realm, by directly influencing the thread of events here on earth. So, similarly, one might be a few minutes early or late, and synchronistically avoid accident due to the care of a departed loved one. Souls in the spiritual world can send us thought forms, feelings and intuitions to protect us from danger -- or even from simple stress and inconvenience. The number of directions in which a series of events might turn or change leans toward the infinite. Any external, physically-based event can conceal, due to humankind's limited capacity to sense much beyond the physical, an endless number of outcomes initiated in the world of spirit. If we have developed sensitivity of soul, the dead can further communicate with us and protect us through acts of grace. Crucial information can be given, and we benefit greatly from the hyper-broadened, supersensible, spiritually-based knowledge of those who have passed. Additionally, someone who has died can instruct us to complete a personal goal they were unable to finish during life, thus completing a project valuable to the world at large. Listen closely to your dreams, and avoid the temptation to discount them -- you may be receiving just such a message.

Those among the living who lack awareness of these synchronicities proceed through life with closed-off or narrowed vision. After death, one realizes and sees all worldly events with omniscient clarity and certainty. If one has really been living anthroposophically during earthly life, one will begin to notice, understand and learn from these occurrences as they manifest. In our time, channels of communication between worlds are flying open at an exponential rate, and whether the resultant psychic impressions come through as clear and distinct or as vague and muted depends wholly upon the current degree of spiritual belief and faith held by the individual.

Physical life on earth manifests as the tiniest part of the macrocosmic universe, while in the spiritual world, after death, we actually expand to become one with the macrocosm. From there, we can easily influence earthly events on the smaller scale. On earth, we have access to memory; in the spiritual world, we possess certainty. The living often exercise a general lack of perception. "Today, people only consider the poverty-stricken sequence of what has actually occurred," while finer influences go unheeded. The options available to us are infinite, however, and favorable moments for the dead to reach us can occur upon receiving messages through dream imagery. Spiritual knowledge can then be transformed directly into actual feeling and experience through intentional prayer, in which heartfelt study opens the pathways of the mind and soul. Additionally, the habit of forming mental images of the afterlife helps us, while we are still in the physical realm, to awaken to communication between the worlds and to the boundless possibilities of the human soul.

In the physical realm, the ego takes authoritative charge of the astral body, and commonly perceives the waking, physical, linear world as the single, obvious, exclusive form of reality. As humans, we are theoretically able to act, according to free will, solely within the parameters of these basic limitations -- but it is not advisable. Because we possess free will in this realm, we can choose to live with zero regard to the spiritual self or to the welfare of others. Astral consciousness can remain, either by conscious or unconscious choice, entirely absent or hidden. Actions negating the welfare of others, however, never unfold without consequence. Whether or not karma appears to engage during physical life, it manifests with absolute certainty after death, causing the soul to feel every ounce of distress it has ever caused another. In the first stage after death, called Kamaloka in Anthroposophy, souls without anthroposophical or spiritual anchor experience a torment of loneliness, because without a reference point, they are unable to get their bearings and gain the attention of other spirits living in the heavenly realm. They drift along as ghosts, unable to reach out. It is clearly preferable to carefully nourish the morality present in our souls while we are still living on earth, in order to avoid such pain.

The astral body, during physical life, can possess a love and longing for spirit of which the ego is fully unaware. Spiritual consciousness, when experienced on the physical plane, does not automatically extend to the physical, astral or etheric elements of our being, or even to our waking awareness. On earth, we can develop and thereby affect only the ego, while the other aspects of ourselves must wait for growth in the spiritual realm. After death, one might crave or wish for elements of spirituality of which one had been ignorant (or even decisively opposed) during life, but experience a complete inability to gain this knowledge alone. During physical life, subconscious longings, even if acknowledged, are rarely lived out to their fullest extent; but "death...transforms untruths into truths," and the wishes and desires we have concealed from ourselves in life will become instantly activated after death. Even during our time on earth, outside spiritual forces can influence the astral body with regard to soul life, causing a leaning toward a line of spiritual thinking heretofore ignored or dismissed. The powers of

11

our souls can change, and what appears outrageous or unbelievable in physical life can become our full reality after death.

In our era, in order to prepare for life after death, we are required to learn essential spiritual truths in a way markedly different from that of our ancestors, because our old means of spiritual orientation—the inherently magical, primeval, inherited knowledge of ancient humanity—no longer exists. It has been gradually erased by the passage of time, and we no longer hold a clear memory from which we could theoretically retrace our steps. A new sense of orientation is necessary, and in the anthroposophical tradition, this involves a deep understanding of Christ, a communication between the worlds and a pure, effortless, infallible kindness during physical life. Throughout earthly life, we must relate to the supersensible world in order to meet the Angels, or Higher Hierarchies, after death and to properly receive knowledge from them. In this way, we are more fully prepared to absorb their deeper teachings of the heavenly realm, thereby bringing spiritual progress to a subsequent life. If we are unable to conceptualize and open up to basic awareness of the angels and heavenly beings during earthly life, we find only impenetrable darkness after death. We may be passed closely by these beings during the course of our journey in the afterlife, but find ourselves completely unable to gain their attention or connect with them.

To facilitate preparation for life between death and rebirth, human beings need to nourish clear-sighted, truthful and unaffected moral consciousness as the overriding, essentially freeing rule by which to live our lives. This will keep our souls open to the heavenly light of the angels as we pass into the next world. Immediately after death, we find the heavenly realms unlit and wholly unnavigable unless we have brought through to them a purity of consciousness; a spiritual sweetness allows the angels to illumine the way for us. Similarly, materialistic thoughts held during life prove terribly detrimental to soul development after death. In fact, such patterns, if carved habitually, repetitively or intentionally into our earthly process, can bring about the undesired consequence of attracting deeply negative forces that seek to use us solely for their purposes. A pronounced lack of conscience during earthly life actually delivers the souls of the dead to become servants of evil beings in the realms that follow. "Everything that happens has a spiritual foundation."

Likewise, speaking an untruth during physical life causes a reciprocal decrease in the purity of the ego and one's own sense of selfworth. Materialistic ideas held during earthly life "incarcerate us in the realm of the spirit," keeping souls thus affected quite invisible, separate and unable to communicate, thereby depriving them of the forces of positive attraction that they would normally need in the planetary spheres. Along our chosen path, whether it be filled with spiritual light or its opposite, we create and form our own karma and line of soul activity. What we bring into the spiritual world from earth matters a great deal. If one takes immoral influences through the gate of death or spends too much time, while living, in criticism of others, one cannot attract the right forces in the next world, and meets only darkness. This is karma explained. The Higher Hierarchies and angelic beings cannot recognize an accumulation of meanness, judgment or negativity around a soul, and must therefore leave it alone, passing it by as if it were quite invisible. The problem for such a soul arises in the harsh realization that the assistance of the Higher Hierarchies is absolutely necessary to their well-being and to that of all souls; without their spiritual goodness and light, the way through the heavens and planetary spheres remains obscured, shadowed and incomprehensible, and the soul loses out, sacrificing still more of its true nature as negative beings and dark spirits move in opportunistically to secure its work and energy for their own purposes.

Equally, a true awareness of our soul nature as an expansive awareness, moving far beyond the mere physical, can lead us to a more spiritual life here on earth, thereby helping to light our way as the soul crosses the heavens. In this case, the earthly incarnation has been lived out well, and the soul has attracted the exquisite gaze of the Divine. One is able to move forward, accumulating wonderful karma that builds upon itself as the soul flies through the heavens. Concurrently, the feeling of "grandeur, of reverent awe" we feel when gazing at a night sky uninterrupted by city lights affects us so profoundly because the stars, where our souls progress toward the next life, are our true and ancient home, our birthplace and source.

Artistic and esthetic beauty, as expressed on earth, are of great importance to the well-being of the conscious psyche but qualify as an outer gesture only, when it comes to the health of the soul. Occult perception, capable of seeing beauty across all existing realms, is enlightened and deepened to a far greater degree than artistic perception, which has its roots firmly planted in the material. Occultism and deep, esoteric and spiritual understanding contribute directly to art in the physical world. The Medici figurines of Michelangelo, for example, "express the life body" in all its forms. During physical life, we can practice discovering that which is spiritually concealed in those closest to us; in other words, their true soul nature, often shrouded by the intense, surface-oriented demands of earthly life. As a result, compassion, understanding and spiritual love pour from us, effectively demonstrating "the power of love in the soul of man."

Our physical surroundings on earth greatly influence the soul while we are here, and as human beings, we are responsible for creating our own conditions of life. Everything of artistic beauty, in fact, "has its origin in the supersensible world," influenced by the working of our souls through previous lives, living in the ancient harmony of the spheres before physical art came into expression on this plane. In our times, a profit-oriented cheapening of our physical surroundings has been instigated by marketing and the widespread perception that affordable things, by necessity, must be of lower quality. Beautiful things are believed to be expensive and out of reach, and this has convinced many to live in esthetically degraded surroundings. Lack of adequate or extended education in art causes mass dissociation with beauty to become the norm; so many people are simply unaware of the possibilities, and do not know that beauty lies within the reach of everyone. An expensive college education is not a prerequisite for artistic study, because anyone, exercising free will, can visit the library and be immersed in giant, colorful volumes of art, discovering along the way a personal esthetic which can then be incorporated into daily life and surroundings. If one has access to free time devoted to reflection in nature, surrounded by the original and perfect beauty of the earth, so much the better.

During physical life, atmosphere matters. The warmth of the soul shines when surrounded by calm and beauty. Honor your own esthetic. For inspiration, check into the innumerable suggestions and recommendations given by Rudolf Steiner in the books and lectures he produced throughout his lifetime. He had a very beautiful way of seeing and describing light and color that allows spiritual light to shine through into the physical, creating radiance in our common sphere.

While on earth, two essential qualities must be cultivated for a peaceful passage into the next life: love for the spiritual world and a state of calm and inner rest, allowing the soul to live peacefully, free of vanity. It is not relevant, in spiritual truth, whether something of great import for the world happens through oneself or through another person; we can evolve spiritually by freeing our minds of the need for excessive attention and recognition during life. Everyone can work as one, toward common goals, and specific revelations will come through those individual souls best suited to bring forward each idea in the fullness of its expression. As we cease to grasp at status and personal recognition in return for public accomplishment, we begin to work uniquely for the good of

15

humankind. In this way, we can enjoy inner rest, and feel glad when another person achieves. This is true selflessness for the good of all, and allows humankind to progress peacefully and without distraction.

The more we try to understand the spiritual world during life, the smoother and more fruitful the transition after death will be. Between lives, we gather strong spiritual forces to "build up to the next earthly existence." Between death and rebirth, our thoughts and feelings exist outside of us, and as we expand, our true identity and center exists only in spiritual consciousness. Images of what we believed and experienced during life surround us, and "we behold as an outer cosmic painting" who we were, during earthly life, as a living person. During that time, we lived within the limits of our skin; after death, we exist throughout and inside of objects and things, permeating everything and sharing space in a most unexpected manner, because the soul has gradually and exponentially expanded into the greater cosmos, growing larger with each major understanding given to it in the afterlife.

Anthroposophy predicts that at the end of human evolution, when our souls have ascended spiritually to the greatest possible height, "our bodily nature will be most barren." The decline of inherited, primeval soul wisdom began at humanity's bodily peak, during the Greek epoch, when humans celebrated the external, the visible, the outer and the physical above all else. This type of "external beauty has no future" now, merely for its own sake. In fact, despite the current, myopic obsession with outer perfection and glamour, inner beauty has become increasingly crucial to the human soul, and must shine forth just like the inner essence of the sun and moon. The education of children, teenagers and adults in Anthroposophy could assist greatly in the healing and removal of cultural, epidemic body dysmorphia, food addiction, anorexia and simple preoccupation with appearance, which only succeeds in setting aside the spiritual self, draining us to emptiness. Through cultivation of spiritual science, we will eventually grasp a greater understanding of the soul's future life, instead of constantly striving for physical excellence, as the ancients did so well in the Greek games. Eventually, humankind will "learn to be independent of what is bound to the physical body," and the importance of gathering for spiritual work will be recognized as a natural and crucially important human practice. We will cultivate consciousness with regard to the preparation of our karma rather than pouring all of our awareness into the physical alone. In our time, many people are still not really aware of the spiritual world, but the afterlife of the soul brings with it the capacity to influence the physical world, and both individual and group consciousness will, with experience and practice, grow over time.

During earthly life, we can receive information from the spiritual world and enliven our souls, receiving great comfort and inspiration; or we can dull ourselves and refuse to perceive essential truths. It is our free choice. No matter how we perceive religion or spirituality, we should not, under any circumstances, allow our innate spiritual powers to wither during life. An open mind is essential. We must continue to ceaselessly cultivate spiritual awareness; otherwise, we do nothing but obliterate ourselves spiritually in later realms, after physical death. If this unfortunate result were to come about, we would exist only as a plucked flower, without roots but never put into a vase of water, unable to receive or process life-giving nourishment and hydration. This is why Anthroposophists gather together to cultivate spiritual science: to prepare the soul for the great crossing-over, so that we may experience some sort of orientation to the life beyond and avoid shocking and unpleasant surprises. Here on earth, we are, in fact, capable of perceiving calls from the spirit world, and of hearing angels and beneficent hierarchical beings telling us directly how to cultivate spiritual truth within the earthly realm. At this point, it becomes a matter of listening intently and well, and then putting our spiritual guidance into practice while we still have the chance.

17

What appears to exist to the waking self during day-to-day earthly consciousness can be quite different from that which actually resides in the soul; people can feel differently about the same matter either before or after death, when everything takes on its "true coloring." If living people have spiritual thoughts, even if they are not anthroposophical in origin, the dead will be able to see and hear them, and thereby become able to communicate with those individuals and help them, or vice-versa. After death, when we meet beings of the Higher Hierarchies and certain other elemental beings, we must be ready to greet them with a brightly-shining light, fully capable of diffusing the darkness of the spirit realm. If we go through physical life carefully excluding any judgment or criticism of others, they will be able to meet these beings far more easily in the next worlds. "Earthly life is not only a transitional stage; it has a mission." The quality of our spiritual life here on earth directly affects our life in the beyond. The light for the afterlife must, in fact, be carried up from earth. There exist unlimited currents between earth and the inhabited heavenly realms that we can activate and bring to life while we are still here, in order to initiate and practice communication and exchange.

Only on earth can we meet certain souls, and these are the loved ones who together comprise the core group of our truest and most meaningful relationships and soul connections. We forge all relationships here, in the physical realm, and merely continue them in the spiritual world, where continuation (and not initiation) of established relationships is the only option. Our connections with others are absolutely rare and precious, the very fiber and nourishment of our spiritual existence, and the soul who has recently passed into the afterlife feels this most intensely, experiencing great joy or regret, sweetness or sorrow, depending upon the quality of relationships they conducted while living on the physical plane.

This same concept applies to relationships of greater community. Spiritually, we must focus upon instilling light in co-creation with other souls while we are still here, so that we can receive impulses from supersensible beings in the beyond and communicate with our friends and loved ones later. This becomes easier with the support of a willing community of like-minded souls. Without any spiritual community previously established during earthly life, a person who had already passed into the next world would have to rely on being intentionally read to (from an anthroposophical or spiritual text) by a loved one still residing in the physical world. In this way, necessary information could be imparted that may have been ignored or omitted while the person was still alive on the earthly plane.

Certain people find themselves unable to find the correct path during earthly life, and for them, heavenly gifts are not properly received from the Higher Hierarchies after death. These souls might exhibit, while still living on earth, narrow-mindedness about spiritual matters; they could live their whole lives as self-centered individuals for whom "nothing fits rightly". For this type of person, "life impinges upon him, and he feels continually wounded." This description directly mirrors the symptoms and characteristics of narcissism, the intractable and insidious psychological condition which, in our time, has exploded to epidemic proportions. If such souls add to these traits a "religious egoistic element" or a fanaticism incapable of open, unbiased spiritual perspective, they further open themselves to the unfavorable influences of negative Arhimanic beings and, as they move through the gate of death, will be under the influence of these spirits in a continuous, increasing cycle of attachment and control. During life, these souls move about "equipped with blinders" that prevent the true cultivation of an open mind and heart. A person like this may be intellectually capable of addressing higher spiritual concepts, but wholly incapable of going beyond rigid religious or psychological boundaries with regard to spirituality. Locked up in a rigidified experience, the soul loses touch with the correct rhythm and pace of the life-death-rebirth cycle. People can therefore experience a diminished ability, intensified with each passing incarnation, to direct the fate of their own soul. Negative influences build up around them, their choices and deeds are marked in their soul records, and karma must then be lived out, both before and after physical death.

Human beings progress spiritually by pursuing real devotion, enthusiasm, and warmth for every one of the tasks we must carry out in service to all humankind. Activities that inspire true, unmodified enthusiasm are far more elusive now than they were in ancient times; therefore, we now have a special social responsibility not only to seek out these activities within the difficult social context of our time, but to inspire other souls to accomplish goals in their lives with enthusiasm, as well. If we are able to grasp, within our earthly reach, true enthusiasm and spiritual accomplishment met with devotion, we acquire the possibility, after death, of becoming servants of God and of carrying out healings alongside the angels and higher spiritual beings. This leads us to peace, acceptance and accomplishment in the afterlife and in all of our next lives, as well.

In everyday life, we may sometimes find ourselves chained to our jobs out of necessity, because we face the stark reality of financially supporting ourselves and our families. In the spiritual sense, however, it is of the greatest importance to feel devotion and enthusiasm for our chosen work, straight from our heart and the truth of our innermost desires. This type of balance prepares the spirit to work in a capacity of goodness and healing in the afterlife.

It is therefore our obligation to ourselves and to the world, if we are to attain the highest possible spiritual condition during life and to provide the greatest possible assistance after death, to find work that actually feeds and brings joy to the soul. This has become a bit easier in recent years with the advent of virtual communication; one is no longer forced to rely solely upon the local economy for income, to travel to a separate physical location for work, or to work under negative or vindictive bosses or supervisors. Many people choose to work from home, thereby freeing themselves to spend time with their families and to follow a more natural rhythm of life. Others begin spiritually oriented businesses or find work in the field most suited to them. If we choose to work in accordance with our deepest spiritual desires, we nurture not only our own highest dreams, but the needs and feelings of our loved ones and the greater community, as well.

While on earth, we must make an effort to adapt to both spiritual and physical life, safeguarding lifelong enthusiasm, love of learning and kindness to others as sacred attributes, while taking exquisite care of our own emotional, physical and spiritual health. We must keep joy at the forefront, making sure that we are willing to complete our necessary work with a self-sufficient, independent, uncomplaining attitude, especially when faced with the mundane tasks of earthly life that everyone has to face. We do well if we are able to remain open to new thoughts and ideas, keeping humor and levity within easy reach. We can only find bliss after death and work with the Higher Hierarchies in the heavenly realms if we have been able to truly adapt ourselves to earthly conditions -- dense, hard and unforgiving as they may be -- and to examine our karma with an open spirit during physical life.

Life on earth is "...a gift, a grace from the spiritual world" to be lived to its fullest, most joyous extent with respect for ourselves and others, as well as planned preparation for the afterlife. In the spiritual world, there is no dissolution, no destruction and no death, but it is quite possible for souls who have passed over to the spirit world to experience intense loneliness if they have not properly prepared for the crossing. This feeling is far more painful than earthly loneliness, and happens most commonly to souls who have not developed empathy toward others during earthly life. In fact, "fear of loneliness is the torment in the spiritual world." To avoid a situation like this in the afterlife, we require a sound moral disposition along with strong religious sensibility and willing reverence during physical life. We may find a path in that direction through an expanded understanding of Christianity, considered by Anthroposophy to be the seed of universal religion.

In complement to Christian study, we can also choose to have faith in our own intuition, psychic ability and spiritual gifts, knowing that over-reliance on a linear perspective or physical science alone always leads to a dead end because "life itself always eludes scientific investigation," and "any understanding of life remains but an ideal for science." This is because all life flows from the supersensory into the physical world. It is important to remember that while living here on earth, we do not yet know ourselves fully; we are limited to the earthly realm, within all of its necessary structures and constructs. In essence, during physical life, we are not yet ourselves; we are simply "preparing to expand into the macrocosm", which contains infinitely more than we can possibly understand from an earthly vantage point.

In the spiritual world, we actually *become* the world around us, and live at one with everything that surrounds us. At the same time, we live within the fullness of ourselves. This one "shattering fact" clarifies the main reason for such careful preparation; for if we are to be able to see the totality of ourselves in the spiritual world, unified and at one with the universe, we must start now to lay the proper karmic pathway. We must work hard to purify and prepare our souls.

Our greatest mission on earth is to establish friendships and connections with loved ones. Anthroposophy tries to act as a foundation for bringing people together to create connections, in preparation for the time beyond the physical. The popular view of heaven, which holds that everything works itself out automatically forever after, is not held by Anthroposophy. Very few souls totally deny religion and the spiritual world while here on earth, and they are even less likely to do so in the moment of death; so the worst-case scenario of utter spiritual desolation actually comes to pass very infrequently.

To be a truly and authentically moral soul, one has to acknowledge that one has a relationship with all human beings. After death, moral souls find connections with other moral souls, and they form groups and communities in the spiritual world just as they do here. After death, the soul enters into experiences formed by religious choices made on earth and total individual karma. The groundwork has been laid by every earthly choice we ever made, in any of our incarnations. We are therefore able to avoid loneliness in the spiritual realm by cultivating religious connections here, while we are still in physical bodies and possessed of the ability to effect change upon our karma.

After passing through the gate of death and moving through the heavenly spheres, we eventually enter into a time when we must comprehend all religions; this is an absolutely essential part of the process as we arc toward our next incarnation. A correct understanding of Christianity, brought through the dying process and into the beyond, opens up the impulse to examine and understand all faiths. In this phase and always, there must be no intolerance toward other religions, only acceptance and open-hearted participation. In any case, Christianity presupposes that everyone has the capability to be inwardly Christian, and the anthroposophical worldview itself serves as an instrument of Christianity, which it considers to be the last of the earthly religions.

The spoken language we use on earth has been adapted to describe only the physical plane, the mental and the sensory, the here and now; so it is, of course, very challenging to accurately describe the spiritual world while we are still living on earth. In fact, the intellect, "bound to the brain, ceases to function after death". Life is irrevocably, utterly different in the spiritual world. We are without moorings. The senses vanish completely, whereas the entirety of our perception had, on earth, been received exclusively through the senses. On the earthly plane, the soul is contained within the density of the physical body; but after death, it leaves that same physical and etheric body, floats up and and grows until it fills the orbit of the moon. From there, it moves on to the spiritual construct of each planet in turn, in order to receive specific areas of karmic growth, before traveling beyond the solar system and out into the greater universe to prepare for reincarnation and rebirth.

For the deceased soul, the physical eyes employed so readily during earthly life correspond with the reception of *feeling* after physical death. In other words, everything we once saw, we now sense or feel through clairsentience, clairvoyance or psychic sight. Feeling is what allows the light in, and what allows us to see after we have died. Materialistic or unkind souls, once they have passed through the gate of death, cannot perceive others very well at all. Actually, they cannot even perceive themselves. They are forced to look back upon earthly life exclusively, and that narrow vision now represents the totality of their external world. They have only their memories, and to a spirit in the next world, this counts for almost nothing; it is completely insufficient with regard to the existence of the soul and the way in which its experience should be lived out.

"The earth is neither a mere transitional stage, nor a veil of despair." Life in the physical world carries far greater import than we may have previously guessed, and the fact that we are ultimately in control of and responsible for our destinies may, for some, come as a further shock. Life on earth "exists so that on it, a spiritual knowledge can be developed which can then be carried upward into the spiritual worlds." The greater our awareness of these facts while we are still here, the easier our time will be once we have passed on. We will still be learning, working and growing, but we will certainly not suffer, emotionally or otherwise.

Extending compassion toward others with great frequency and reliability, while simultaneously raising our awareness of what this feels like in our hearts, represents the first step along this path. "Each human soul must be to us a sacred riddle," and it is up to us to spiritually explore the psyche of another in an effort to understand how we may provide for them. The secrets of the cosmos are thereby intimately connected with the secrets of the human being. We must find the ability to recognize the person standing before us as one of us, and silence all prejudice we may feel ceasing to judge; because never can we understand the totality of another person's feeling, experience or logic. According to the law of free will, only that person can direct it, and one never knows which set of hardships, or divine or earthly circumstances, have led to a current situation. We must protect ourselves psychically and use good common sense about people, but refrain from judgment. "True social love" is "the fruit of true spiritual knowledge". We now know that the attitude we choose to hold within ourselves during earthly life directly sows the seeds for our moral and spiritual future, allowing for the creation of our karma over the arc of the heavens.

CHAPTER II

Anthroposophy as Spiritual Nourishment: Reading to the Dead

One of the assumptions of anthroposophical philosophy lies in the belief that one need not be clairvoyant to experience communication with the other side. "New discoveries can be made all the time" by anyone, especially if we have made reference to Anthroposophy or spiritual science, considered to be the spiritual "lifeblood of the soul". As a system of belief, Anthroposophy exists as a reality, not a theory; Steiner saw and received with clairvoyant perception, in real time, its tenets and truths. It is a balm for the soul, a "true life elixir" for people seeking to better their lives, iron out their karma, or communicate with a deceased loved one. One of the tasks of Anthroposophy has historically been to inspire spiritual enthusiasm during physical life, thereby increasing the chances of a spiritually nourished individual and a smooth, effective transition into the realms beyond. With the current, accelerated psychic evolution of humanity, the spiritual world is gradually becoming more accessible to all, and can thus creatively impact our lives with greater ease. Many are able to see through to the other side, who never considered themselves particularly clairvoyant before, because Anthroposophy provides clear instructions for doing so, along with detailed descriptions of the afterlife, the Higher Hierarchies and Jesus.

During our time in the earthly realm, it is our responsibility to "enliven the impulse toward spiritual science" and make a special effort to let it be important to our lives in a balanced way, without allowing it to override all else. It is, of course, perfectly alright and even preferable to enjoy being in a physical body, to drink in and savor life on earth to the fullest; but we must also acquire distinct knowledge of the spiritual world in order to prepare for death, and this can be done through Anthroposophy. If we study spiritual

27

science during physical life, we will, once we have died, find ourselves able to share a common spiritual language with those still living, and to initiate communication between worlds, thereby reaching our dearest loved ones who have been left behind in the physical realm. The soul's pathway through the stars will be complete and well lit by the Higher Hierarchies, allowing us to move through essential development and growth.

The importance of spiritual communities such as the anthroposophical one, when it comes to the place of faith in one's life, cannot be underestimated. "Living together and getting in touch" is of paramount importance for experiencing a successful transition into the next world, because it creates a spiritual community extending beyond the boundary of physical death. It opens the possibility of communication between the worlds and thus prevents loneliness in Kamaloka, the first, sometimes confusing, temporary state of existence we experience after crossing over.

On earth, the refreshing, elemental quality of nature also provides profound inspiration for the soul, due to the inherent perfection and exquisite beauty of all that is directly created by God. A walk in the woods, according to Anthroposophy, represents an experience far closer to spiritual reality than anything we could intentionally devise, because as humans, we habitually create our own, reliable obstacles to enlightenment. Churches and religious systems are not immune to interference by the darker side of the ego, and no man-made construct can truly compare with the breathtaking cathedral offered by nature.

During earthly life, people who experience strong revelations with regard to the supersensible worlds often feel an urgent necessity to speak about their visions, experiences and epiphanies. This is actually a very serious spiritual matter, and must always be supported and encouraged, never forgotten, diminished or neglected. If someone wants to describe a dream, communication or insight, listen patiently; and likewise, if you have a premonition or vision of your own, write it down, tell someone you trust, and give it credence. In the grand scheme of things, the physical realm is only "of the minutest importance" when compared with the infinity of all that exists, and it behooves us to gain as much understanding as we possibly can, of the other side, while we are still here on earth.

The physical and spiritual worlds have, in our time, been effectively severed by culturally induced materialism, producing a profound block to spiritual sight; but in the future, there can exist a "bridge between the worlds" through Anthroposophy and spiritual science. Prayer and meditation focused specifically upon the phase between death and rebirth can help us to awaken to our own consciousness of larger universal truths. Simple external examination and linear thought, on the other hand, cannot provide all the answers to the infinity of time, space and reality. Anthroposophy actually provides a much broader series of answers than physical science is capable of producing, because exclusive study of the physical considers and analyzes only a narrowly defined part of the whole picture.

Because secret spiritual longings of the soul so often rise to the surface only after someone has died, reading anthroposophical texts to the dead can assist them in the avoidance of loneliness should they find themselves unconnected in the afterlife. Choose any original series of lectures on spirituality by Rudolf Steiner, and read them aloud or silently, as if to yourself, all the while holding a very strong image and feeling of the person who has passed. Form a picture in your mind's eye of your loved one, and make it is vivid as you possibly can; keep it intently in your consciousness while reading. Those of us still living in the physical realm can also talk with the dead in our thoughts, even without a prepared text. Trust your intuition. Everyone has it to a certain degree, and it will improve with openness and practice. You will know when you have received a sign from the beyond, because such symbols are usually so beautiful, clear and obvious that the only thing barring us from believing is our own skepticism. Forget everything you have been taught in this area. Communication with the dead can and does happen all the time; and through Anthroposophy, the living and the deceased can find great comfort. If your departed loved one has been living in darkness due to inattention to spiritual matters during life, they will receive this help "with the utmost gratitude". Spiritual science can assist in tearing down the walls between the living and the dead, providing a medium by which communication becomes definite, clear and wholly possible.

During Kamaloka, the phase right after death, it is impossible for the soul to make new connections; it must continue with the old ones, and may need to be read to by a loved one or a friend if there has indeed been a neglect of soul work during physical life. The dead cannot independently find connections to instruct and guide them in spiritual matters after death; they can only meet deceased individuals they knew while living on earth, and even this can only happen if they have previously followed a spiritual path on the physical plane. Through Anthroposophy, we can experience communication in both directions between the living and the dead, effectively providing spiritual relief for those who have passed; and for those still in the physical realm, this "will bring the supersensible world into the immediate present."

Clairvoyants can provide expertise with regard to gaining insight into the realm of the dead and facilitating communication between the two worlds. As long as the average person remains focused solely upon the use of the five senses in the physical world, they automatically override the natural, intuitive sixth sense, and the spiritual world remains largely hidden; but the clairvoyant can follow the passage between death and rebirth, and assist in episodes of clear communication with trained precision. The two realms, in actuality, are intimately connected, and someone who is practiced at navigating this path can often be of help, depending upon the circumstances surrounding the departed one's earthly situation.

In an account handed down by Steiner from the beginnings of Anthroposophy in Europe, a certain man who had passed through the gate of death was found by a clairvoyant to be in a state of great spiritual pain. He said, "I used to live with those who I have left behind...they shone like rays of the sun." He related that his wife was like sunshine, her words a blessing, but he could not find her now—to him, she appeared unable to speak, as if they had no common language. The two souls felt terribly severed. The man had been blissfully happy in his family life on earth, and could recall every detail of it; but when he awoke after death, he could not find his loved ones. He lived in the spiritual world, and longed to be reunited with his family on earth, but his living family did not follow spiritual science and therefore did not think to seek spiritual connection with him. Unintentionally, they left him desolate due to a lack of spiritual knowledge and consciousness. The clairvoyant was compelled to seek and assist, but not even a psychic could have comforted this man. According to divine law, the presence of love within an earthly connection or relationship is the sacred substance, the glue, the transmitting device required to bring spiritual comfort to a bereaved, departed soul. In this way, family members, friends and loved ones play a much larger role than they may have anticipated when it comes to healing connections broken by physical death, and actually hold a very high degree of restorative power. They are able to comfort, calm and free souls trapped in sadness and fear.

If the man described above had studied Anthroposophy during physical life, he would have shared a common spiritual language with his loved ones and therefore been able to initiate communication between worlds. He would also have been able to find comfort for his soul independently, without relying upon anyone else to first reach out to him. "Souls devoid...of spiritual life encounter many obstacles," and the spiritual pain of the dead creates a demand for increased spiritual fluency among the living. When all is revealed after death, connection with others actually represents one of the "deepest longings of humanity". Those who have experienced hearing the call of the dead are the "pioneers of a future...founded on the cognition of the spiritual worlds."

Without proper comprehension of such a call, people living on earth run the risk of crossing over to the other side "spiritually dumb". Earth is the only place where we can develop spiritually and prepare for the next existence after death; and a healthy spiritual life here leads to ease of communication with other deceased souls after we have crossed. In spiritual health, we keep the ability to reach out to those still living, as well. These two factors, taken together, essentially allow us to retain all social capacity in the worlds beyond. The spiritual sciences are available as tools used to span the gap between the physical and the spiritual realms, to reach an understanding between disparate realities both before and after one has crossed over. Christ's mystical role in the Mystery of Golgotha and the tenets of Anthroposophy exist as linked, communal means toward the expanded, interdimensional communication so vitally important for every soul.

In gathering together to pray and thereby strengthen connections between the two realms, it becomes entirely possible to hear calls from spirit world. We can also clearly hear the hierarchical beings -- the angels and archangels -- teaching us how to expand our spiritual awareness during earthly existence. As we consider the life of the human soul between death and rebirth, we begin to understand that our possibilities during that time are completely dictated by the choices we have made while living. It is so easy to think, while we are here on earth, that we will somehow get to our spiritual growth later, when we have time, or after certain milestones have been reached in our lives. Quite the opposite is true. We must take hold of the present moment, release fear, doubt, worry or hesitation, and begin now. Simply breathing intentionally can work wonders -- why not take a few deep, healing breaths right now, as you read this book? Breathing stops time for a moment, allows us to think and intuit clearly and, most importantly, to feel. We have crucial work to do in the next worlds, as well, and we must be ready and able to absorb the truths of the hierarchies while passing profound spiritual tests. If we are successful, we can advance between successive planetary spheres and move toward our next incarnation and rebirth relatively seamlessly. Humanity is approaching a period when it absolutely must know about spiritual awareness in order to successfully pass between the worlds after physical death. In ancient times, human souls retained spiritual perception throughout physical life, but our access to this knowledge has arrived at a state of complete dilution, and creative work on this front is needed.

In the future, it will be normal to communicate with the dead and, in turn, to receive communication from them. A channel of light and understanding will arise between the worlds, and a deep working understanding will become prevalent between the living and the dead, stripped of its current veils and barriers. Between five and eight years after death, though sometimes earlier, even language barriers cease to exist for the deceased;the person who has crossed can now understand languages he or she did not speak in life, and all linguistic communication becomes unified and intelligible. This assists greatly in the general broadening of understanding, so that souls from both realms can help one another consistently, in all possible ways.

The reading of anthroposophical texts to the dead gives beautiful results, and it is a sweet consideration, one of the "greatest deeds of love that can be performed." The living are the only ones who can effectively soothe the dead if they find themselves disconnected, and they can do this simply by reading anthroposophical works aloud to the departed, just as if they were there sitting in the same room with them. While reading to deceased loved ones, one can be assured that they will listen intently; a clairvoyant can confirm this if there is any doubt. With that said, a family member who has just discovered anthroposophy will actually be better able to read to the dead than a clairvoyant who has had no affectionate connection with the deceased during physical life. Human affection and genuine love are embodied as the divine essence necessary for communication between the worlds. Clairvoyants sometimes read to the dead even if they have not known them during life, but effective communication in these cases often proves difficult.

Anthroposophy exists as a universal language. "When spiritual science really takes hold of the souls of men, the walls between the worlds will crumble." It is the feeling of this inner soul experience that is so important, rather than intellectual thoughts centered around the concept, and for this same reason, a walk in nature can often put us closer to our personal spiritual reality than formal church worship. We have established that spiritual science can only be learned on earth; but at the same time, each subsequent planetary realm has its own lessons that can only be learned in that particular place. Spiritual science is also the only way to gain connection with the higher worlds; no other existing means can support it so well. Even if someone has not been open to Anthroposophy until this very moment in life, there is still the chance to do just as much good; and, barring that, there will also be the chance to return to earth and experience it at a later stage. There is, therefore, no need to despair or worry if someone cannot accept Anthroposophy at any given time.

A single means of healing communication with the spiritual world exists, and that is through the living -- people who have had some form of attachment with a soul during earthly life. If a person dies

34

with no knowledge of Anthroposophy and has no family members reaching out psychically, knowledge of it can still be gained by way of connection with a living acquaintance familiar with spiritual science, someone known during life on earth. This is an indirect manner of gaining communication, but it is possible. If they have no spiritual community at all, the dead will have to rely on being spontaneously read to by a loved one or acquaintance, but this is a bit like the children's story *Sylvester and the Magic Pebble* by William Steig, in which a donkey finds a wishing stone and suddenly wishes to become invisible to a hungry lion, but then finds himself unable to reconnect with his bereft family until they spontaneously (and unexpectedly) wish him back into his original form while holding the same magic stone he had used. Alternatively, if an anthroposophist is given a handwriting sample of another anthroposophist who has died, that person can also read to the dead quite effectively, even if the two did not know one another during earthly life. It is incredibly satisfying to be a part of a spiritual group or community that can facilitate communication from many different standpoints and avenues.

It is relatively common, even for anthroposophists, to sometimes find themselves intensely distracted by the physical world and all that occurs here; after all, the five senses dominate our earthly perception, and the pull of the dense and the physical is very strong indeed, to the point of temporarily overtaking spiritual sight. With the passage of time, though, anyone who is willing can move on to deeper levels of the soul and become able to help the dead more effectively. An anthroposophist who goes through the gate of death and brings along spiritual thoughts, can also act in service to the dead from the other side, even taking on a leadership role among them, but this can prove quite complicated. It is actually easier to accomplish such goals from the earthly realm.

The soul, in the world beyond, finds itself entirely dependent upon, and obedient to, previous earthly connections even if the connection has been tense, dramatic or oppositional. Even if two people held opposite views during life, they will be able to understand each other after one of them has died, through the practice of reading to the dead. Once the second person dies, however, the difficulty between them begins again, when they find themselves once more on equal footing. When the two souls are again connected, a remembrance of earthly life takes place, and dissonance can manifest once again, because both souls are entirely dependent upon that which had previously passed between them".

Given a connection that is spiritually open, the dead can also work on us here, in the earthly sphere; events of physical life are "strung on a thread" in their vision, and can be foreseen, influenced and deeply understood from the vantage point of the other side. It has often been said that the dead have simultaneous vision, and can keep track of all of their loved ones at the same time. In the modern sense, it is almost as though they have many screens from which to keep watch -- spiritual screens filled with images of all of our everyday happenings, joys, sorrows, trials and tribulations. The external content of earthly life -- that which is normally visible to us using the five senses -- actually represents just a fraction of the totality of possible consciousness. It is easy for our departed loved ones to see everything clearly if they have led a spiritually-based life. In actuality, infinite inner possibilities exist behind the facade of physical events. Behind them, an "entire world of possibilities" exists, and can lie untapped without spiritual understanding. Additionally, much of what *could* happen, sometimes in the negative sense, never comes to pass because divine or spiritual forces intercede to set things right. Because of our general lack of awareness of this fact, "we are continually led by...possible events that do not actually happen," such as assuming that we need to be punctual, only to find out later that the opposite was true. Wonderful opportunities can arise precisely because we were stopped in our tracks or diverted by an unknown force. In reality, only the visible aspect of one's appearance changes after death; souls who have moved on are still alive and well, but once Kamaloka passes, they are busy moving forward through successive phases of intense spiritual growth. Most people only live on the surface of physical life, but the dead have a sweeping, eagle's eye view over the tiniest intricacies and workings of our world. As a counterpoint to this realization, consider that conditions available only to the clairvoyant, at present, will gradually become "a common heritage for the whole of humanity", and that we will eventually develop the prescience and psychic ability to forecast world events, as well.

With that said, lack of belief in the spiritual world creates a gigantic hindrance to those who could otherwise have easily established faith while living in the earthly realm and benefitted from such connections. Even a clairvoyant can intermittently be limited by the common lack of belief inherent to so many, and find themselves able to see unreliably -- only sometimes, and without predictable outcome. Spiritual science offers to us a life-giving impulse, and we have the opportunity to constantly strive to increase our level of faith, feeling and love of God in order to help the future of humanity. It is our responsibility to uphold Anthroposophy, and direct it so that it may guide both living and transitioning souls as they travel between the worlds. If we succeed, and spiritual science can wash in a healing wave over all aspects earthly consciousness, "humanity will experience an awakening from the sleep of life."

Reading to the dead need only be done in thought, on the psychic level, and reading aloud is not at all required. There exists no rigid format in which this must be done, no fixed plan which must be followed; it is the internal love and feeling emitted by the reader, as well as the anthroposophical nature of the text, that is important. Human beings in the physical world can have a highly impactful healing effect on souls in the spiritual world with regard to projects left undone or incomplete, and can help them finish what they cannot now do for themselves, having crossed over to a different world where the rules have changed.

Departed souls sometimes run into difficulty imparting messages, protection and healing to souls in the earthly realm, because so many people here live exclusively in "I" or ego consciousness, and possess voluntary awareness only of the simple laws and predictable occurrences of the physical world. Here on earth, we generally notice what *happens*, but not what *could* happen; and the latter is infinitely greater in scope, especially when one considers the widened, opened-up perception of time and space accessed by the dead. In the spirit world, *possibilities exist as forces,* and such psychic experiences can even happen to human beings living in the physical world when these forces penetrate through to our earthly awareness. In reality, the life of spirit world is completely interwoven with ours here in the physical realm, though we may not always realize it. There exists a "super-abundance of spiritual life behind our physical life", and as we begin to allow our ideas, concepts and expectations to become open and receptive through anthroposophical thought, we gain a true sense of all available possibilities.

Only when we intimately know and understand how Anthroposophy affects life on earth can it create a connection between the physical and spiritual worlds. With the passage of time, people have become more and more open and aware of the spiritual world, and it will eventually become quite natural to access regular psychic communication with those who have passed. Anthroposophy acts as a means to gather information, impressions and knowledge from those with whom we were connected when they were living. Communication between the worlds acts to create an "amplification of human life", an enhancement of our usual experience, but Anthroposophy must hold a place of vitality within our hearts in order for this to happen.

Materialism often prevents full actualization of the relationship between the soul and the body. It is easy to be distracted by the outer appearance and physical machinations of external life. In his lectures on life between death and rebirth, Steiner made the brilliant comparison with a wristwatch; simply put, the mechanism by which we measure time actually has nothing to do with time itself -- the reality of time, and the place it holds in universal consciousness. The watch is merely the physical means by which time may be measured, quantified and viewed. Similarly, materially based awareness may cause the soul to feel forgotten or disconnected from the body -- but only as long as we remain preoccupied only with the physical. The soul, of course, holds within it the totality of who we are, and this awareness cannot be kept at bay for long. When we open up our sensibilities and perception to the higher realms, it becomes easy to see that both the soul and the physical body must live in a harmonious connection, and that this will etch into the future a capacity for independence in the realms beyond.

Over the course of the last century or so, a sixth Post-Atlantean age has been prepared through the vehicle of Anthroposophy: an age of new and holistic thought, of spiritual awareness and compassion as a natural, ingrained human characteristic. A "continual deepening of the understanding of the Christ impulse" has come to pass, permeating our consciousness ever more deeply with the passage of time. The light of Christ surrounds us if we are open and aware, and we can invite Him into our souls just by calling Him through prayer or spiritual sight. In the West, the archetypal story of the Holy Grail mystery has been embedded in human consciousness for centuries, and its re-exploration can bring to the modern person an understanding of life between death and rebirth that is appropriate and understandable for our time.

Steiner, in his era, felt that the soul's powers of spiritual perception were in decline, and for this reason he founded

Anthroposophy, a new movement toward enlightened spiritual thought. In the early 1900s, when he was most actively lecturing and touring, human beings remained markedly proud of perceiving only through the physical senses, thereby validating an exclusive commitment to scientific data. In the time following his, he predicted, "man will only be interested in the sub-sensible," and become even more interested in microscopic data -- for example, "what vibrates and oscillates beneath" color. We must be careful, however, because what we are then examining is not color itself, but that which is perceived to lie beneath it. This example can apply to countless areas of modern scientific advancement, including recent changes around the genetic modification of food. Steiner, as always, was prescient. Scientists in the postmodern age may only be interested in what is *behind* nature, but continued advancement in these areas alone, without attention to the whole picture, can only result in the degradation of the earth, of our physical health and even of our inner, spiritual lives.

Anthroposophy exists to work against this sort of mindset in every way possible, wishing instead to give a spirited quality to the human soul, to allow it to live freely in a world unfettered by dogma and restriction. Color and the beauty of one's surroundings are very important for the building of a good self-concept and the courage to explore artistically, intellectually and spiritually. Healthy food remains essential for our physical and spiritual well-being, no matter how modern and advanced the time in which we live. When the proper channels in the psyche are opened, the soul sends to the body a means by which to perceive the world in a spiritual way. Spiritual health, which is supported by physical health, can expand our lives immensely, and many doors can open with the introduction of just one new idea. We must try to do everything we can to remain on an enlightened path, even while still present in earthly life.

It is devastating for a soul, while in the spirit world, to look at the future body, ready for reincarnation, and realize that it is insufficient, that something is missing because of poor choices made in one's previous incarnation. This is felt as a punishment, and in turn causes the spiritual body to lose quality and tone. To avoid this situation, we can commit to opening ourselves to receiving transmissions from the spiritual world while we are still here on earth, through Anthroposophy. Spiritual science gives *life*, an "inward vitality and activity". It represents a possibility for preparation for the afterlife, and humankind has been destined to approach such a line of thought. If someone refuses Anthroposophy in this lifetime, it cannot necessarily be recouped to an equal extent later, but that soul will still have a chance in the next life because there will be more anthroposophical awareness on earth by that time.

Life between death and rebirth "is absolutely a continuation of life here". If they are sensitive, people will notice that their departed loved ones surround them constantly; and if they remain open, they can receive visions and messages from the beyond through spiritual sight. If signs or messages from a departed loved one fail to appear right away, do not despair; sometimes those left behind are still in too much shock, pain and trauma to perceive a sign, and this is completely normal. The rawness and extreme pain of a recent death often has to calm down and heal a bit before communication can occur. This takes time. Practice exquisite self-care, pray, and ask for guidance.

If it is only perceived as an external science, Anthroposophy remains incomplete. It is important not so much to know the details of the afterlife, but to be able to change our lives; not just to know, but "to know with feeling". Anthroposophy brings the spiritual and the material into harmony. It allows us to be "connected in soul with the higher world" even as our world becomes increasingly material over time.

Anthroposophy was created to impart and embody pure spiritual truth, and therefore does not skimp on the facts when it comes to an accurate, unvarnished description of the various forces at play in both realms. Negative spirits also surround us, waiting for a chance to interfere in the life of the soul if we stray in any way from compassion, goodness and spiritual love. *The Guardian of the Threshold* was a theatrical piece created by Steiner to show that we cannot form a simplistic idea about aspects of the "character of Luciferic beings; they can only be gradually learned when we approach them from various aspects" and "observe how they intervene in human life". To know of the presence of such beings does not imply that we are giving them undue or inappropriate recognition or attention; it simply means that we are informed. One might visit the doctor, for example, to receive a diagnosis, so that one can understand and eliminate a disease; but this does not mean that we worship the disease, or that we succumb to it just because we have recognized it. We simply need to know what exists, so that we can deal with it in the proper manner.

Anthroposophy, in the early 1900s, was not yet widely recognized; but it eventually brought great meaning and spiritual awakening to the modern age, in areas ranging from farming and education to spiritual thought. We can therefore endeavor to approach anthroposophical work solely with a "spirit of earnestness and truthfulness". We cannot sum it up in just a few ideas, in a limited sound byte or span of time; it is deep work, and it takes the "whole life of the soul" to comprehend and encompass all of its concepts. In our age, there is so much to distract us and lead us away from the path of truth; corrupt influences are everywhere, vying to steal their share of our attention, and it is necessary to constantly approach spiritual work from a fresh point of view, returning anew to essential concepts time and again. In this way, a reawakening of the soul can take place with each return to the ideas and precepts, and the soul becomes more accustomed, over the years, to the anthroposophical way of life.

To help us understand, we can pursue further reading in the Four Gospels, which can be taken as a "model of how to approach the great truths of existence from different sides." Each gospel represents an opportunity to approach the Mystery of Golgotha, or crucifixion of Christ, from a different aspect—and though we can never know it completely, it helps to have spiritual guideposts as we journey forward. In Anthroposophy, we must "live into" spiritual facts rather than just think about them intellectually. In Steiner's lectures, because of time, it was "impossible to give all that may be said" with regard to Anthroposophy, but it is important to delve still further in, to "learn to work thoroughly and seriously, and really strive" to understand all of the knowledge and profound moral truths brought through us from the spiritual worlds. This preparation of the soul is essential, and the nature of the worlds that meet us after death can sometimes be glimpsed during physical life through the process of initiation. On the physical plane, we are active, constantly moving, using our hands to create, to carry and bring; but in the spiritual world, we find everything reversed, and quite the opposite of what we are used to. There, we remain perfectly still, and knowledge must come to us through the stillness and peace we carry in our souls. Whatever does come to pass is given purely by grace, through no action of our own. From our place in this new spiritual life, we understand this fact completely.

The year 1899 is remembered in Anthroposophy as pivotal, as it marked an "inner soul awakening" for all humankind. It was a year when all of the powers and beings of the spiritual world cooperated with initiates here on Earth; and was the year the end of a 5,000-year cycle called the smaller Kali Yuga came about. This represented a massive turning point in human consciousness, especially with regard to Theosophy as it had evolved by the turn of the twentieth century. Human beings were, from that point forward, obliged to allow souls to approach them in a different manner; realizations and epiphanies "could not come from the outside in such a striking way" as they had in past times. They now had to arrive through the inner

43

self, "from the highest and most interior forces of the soul." The angels, archangels and higher beings needed something from humankind in order to bring Kali Yuga to an end; that was the capacity for human revelation to occur within our souls and thoughts, and for our actions to shine as a reflection of this inner process. In this way, proper cooperation between the worlds could continue through the year 1900 and beyond.

As earthbound human beings, we must not just keep ourselves superficially busy within the span of our days, but should instead approach spirituality and gain enlightenment through an overriding, inherent sense of inner peace. Our contribution to the current state of the world and to the relationship between the two dimensions can be summed up in a state of simple quietude -- to take on an internal sweetness which will, in turn, open up our clairvoyant consciousness. With this simple impulse, we have the ability to strive for a "conscious, grace filled attitude toward the higher worlds."

Just as an artist cannot do his or her best work by simply putting on a great show of being busy, neither can we, by rushing about, hope to achieve communication with the spiritual world. We must instead nourish fertile ground for our own spiritual patience, waiting in acceptance and peace so that signs from the beyond may find their way to us. Psycho-spiritual and energetic healing such as naturopathy or anthroposophical medicine, for which physical medicine is merely the preparation, can help any individual to bring about the state of rest and balance necessary to promote work in the spiritual world. In our time, we will find that "the soul need only be receptive," and that we need only ask the angels and archangels for their assistance. They are the messengers of God, and can only respond if we ask them for help in earnest.

CHAPTER III

Guidelines for Reading to the Departed

Reading to the dead in the anthroposophical sense might at first seem deceptively easy, but there are a few considerations to note, and proper attention to these will render your efforts more effective. First, if no love existed between you and the departed, it makes very little sense to extend the energy. Love is the absolute keystone to the process, the only path by which the reading will bear fruit.

Whether the departed is a close family member or a distant relative, individualized reading scenarios present themselves. Was there a favorite room, for example, in which the individual spent most of their time: a den or library, a playroom for children, a garden or sun room for those who loved the outdoors? Try to figure out the place they loved most for relaxing and passing the time. It is a common experience to visit a home, perhaps to attend a dinner, and notice an inherent coziness and warmth -- while at other houses we feel nothing, perhaps even a cold detachment. True and loving relationships will leave a spiritual imprint upon a room or home. The Japanese call it *kami*, or heart, and that is exactly what it is: a vibrational signature left in the room where the departed spent the most time in a state of comfort, security and love.

Determine that particular room for your family member, and find a comfortable place to sit, maybe on their favorite chair or couch. Tell others in the home that you do not wish to be disturbed during your reading time. Find the book you want to read, perhaps drawing from the suggestions at the end of this volume in the resource section. Alternatively, you might initially choose to read some of their favorite books to them, in order to establish an initial connection across the worlds. Relax, and take a few minutes to let your body calm down from the stress of the day. As you gently

45

breathe, begin to access warm memories of the departed doing what they loved to do best, something specific that will create an energetic frame of reference between you and the memory. You may read silently, or out loud in a soft, gentle voice. Center your feeling in your heart and read from that place, just as if the individual were there with you, sitting across the room. Intone the readings with vibrations of love, and let the departed know that you are reading to them specifically.

If you are a woman with a strong feeling of love for the departed, you will begin to feel a connection with the passage of time. It is said that women are born of the heart, and are far more attuned to the true spiritual essence of love than most men. In this aspect, you may well succeed where men fail.

Feel free to carry on a heartfelt conversation with your loved one. Tell them how much you love them, and how much you miss them in your life. Explain to the departed that you want to help them gain a stronger spiritual foothold in the next life, and that you will be reading to them in the future. Try not to extend your feelings in sadness; reach out with a sense of joy and gratitude, knowing that you are doing something few people have the opportunity to understand, let alone actualize. You are not required to understand how or why this works. You have only to trust, deep down, that you have had a connection with this individual in life and wish to share the same love in death.

Remember that you are expanding the spiritual education of the departed. Do not spend a large amount of time on novels or fiction books; you want to hit the ground running with material that will benefit them. Whether you choose anthroposophical lectures or works of the great Christian mystics, make sure your message is coherent, clear and imbued with kindness.

For those suffering the loss of a child, the devastation will certainly be even more difficult to deal with, because there is always the sense of precious opportunity lost and an unfinished life that ended too young. In actuality, the chronological age of the child who died no longer exists, in the spiritual sense. You are reading to an old soul who has lived countless lives and will go on to live countless more. If the child had a favorite playroom or toys, bring these surroundings near to you for comfort as you read. Feel the child in your arms, recall all the love and warmth they brought into your life, speak to them from your soul and tell them they mean everything to you. Although the pain is unbearable now, you want to share this love with them so their next life will be full of joy and spiritual evolution. Commonly, with the loss of a child, parents' faith in God is severely tested. There is no rational, earthly sympathy that will comfort the soul of a bereft parent, and there is no pain in life greater than the loss of a child. Only time and love will bring healing.

As you sit in their favorite room surrounded by the things loved most by the child, you could begin by reading to them some of their favorite bedtime stories, or books they enjoyed having read aloud. As you read, explain that you will be with them in love, will keep them always in your heart, and wish to help them move on to greater spiritual experiences. You do not have to read every day; read when you feel a heaviness in your heart, and need to share the love that was theirs while they were living. It is advisable to read aloud to children, in the same comforting tonality you would use to read a bedtime story.

Let the words vibrate in your heart as you keep images of your dear one in your mind, and spiritually project your words and love out to them in the ethers. Imagine and visualize a brilliant highway of sparkling light, a path of pure love connecting you to your child. Imagine your words traveling down this path, which connects directly with your child's heart. After a time of reading, you will feel in your heart an indescribable connection with your child, and you will know that your readings are reaching their soul with the help of your deep love.

If the departed is a friend or more distant relative, simply choose a favorite location for you, somewhere that makes you feel comfortable and relaxed. Spend some time relaxing, thinking of your friendship and the times you spent together. Either verbally or inwardly, tell them what you will be doing. Tell them how much their love meant to you in life, and that you want to return that love by reading to them and helping them overcome any difficulties that they may have built up in this lifetime. Ask them to open their heart to yours. Communicate that you will be reading on a regular basis and that they can choose to take in the information you send. In this way, they can receive in gratitude some of the benefits that the Hierarchies are able to bestow upon departed souls.

It is of paramount importance that there be love when reading to the departed. If you are having a bad day or are too stressed out, skip a day. Do not impose stress upon the departed soul. This is just as important for your peace of mind as it is for the departed. You will find, over time, that the love you send out will be sent back to you a hundredfold, and will become instrumental in the healing of your own heart. You are providing a beautiful service for the loved one and for yourself. Never doubt yourself, and never doubt that you are helping the departed. You will find that your answer, ultimately, rests within your own heart.

CHAPTER IV

"I" Consciousness and Awareness of the Self

Consciousness, as it exists within us on the earthly plane, can best be defined as the awareness that enters into the soul every morning upon waking. When we are asleep, we are elsewhere, dreaming, and the "I" wanders: the identity fades, travels, migrates and unravels. Upon waking, all is recouped, and we quickly reassume our working earthly identity. Likewise, the essential "I" consciousness forms a linking continuum between the worlds, remaining intact throughout and between all lifetimes. Our souls can always recognize themselves, of course, while in the realm of spirit; and in precious instances, glimpses and flashes can come through even after reincarnation into another physical body, allowing the individual to understand our role and existence on earth in previous lifetimes.

"I" awareness begins in physical life at the age of three, and is ingrained by means of minor injury, touch, or any experience that presses inward upon the consciousness. Awareness of the self is initiated by "resistance from the world outside", but the "I" also "impacts its own body inwardly" through internal intellectual and spiritual growth. In the life of a young person, meaning gradually comes into the light as the child grows older and more aware. The difference between the true ego and consciousness of our earthly ego begins to surface. The true ego is, amazingly, already active at birth. A child therefore starts out by using his or her own name to refer to the self instead of the word "I"; Consciousness of the ego is still pure and unaware, and the soul is magnanimous, at one with the outer view of the whole rather than just the self-contained view. Before this time in childhood development, it was impossible to actually experience the self in the ego. Afterwards, it becomes possible due to "collision with the outer world"; for example, bumping into things and having either sharp or gentle collisions with the world outside the physical body. We learn, in this way, to distinguish the self from the outer world as children. Even as teenagers and adults, the ego can only be maintained and kept active (which is essential to the healthy continuance of our soul) through further collisions experienced throughout our earthly existence.

Upon awakening each morning, the ego impacts both daytime reality and inner life, repetitively pushing against the physical and etheric body from all sides and thus affecting us, cumulatively and continually, with each passing day. This causes a gradual wearing away process on the body that can be directly equated with the process of aging. The soul, if all goes well, continues to expand and calm with age, bringing an increasing state of peace; but the body cannot indefinitely withstand the wear and tear of daily life without consequence, and begins to weaken, soften and change. With that said, "I" consciousness does not extend automatically to the physical, astral or etheric being—it can really only affect ego, and develop it.

As we have seen, that which comprises the "I" and the astral body disappears during sleep, and reappears in the morning when both of these return to rejoin the physical and etheric body. We keep our "I" consciousness active by coming into contact with our inner being each morning. This repeated event acts as a collision between the ego and the physical body, and each re-entry contributes to the gradual wearing away of the body over the course of a lifetime. "We collide with our body...and thereby destroy it." Ideas emerge, upon waking, from the depths of consciousness, and these concepts can be preserved in memory. This phenomenon can be highly impersonal and random, a mere transmission of information from the outer worlds having very little to do with the self. All that is held in memory is therefore capable of liberating itself from the ego. In this way, it is possible to experience the pure ego yet again, unaltered by time and our present incarnation.

We remain squeezed into our physical bodies throughout the day, and the counter pressure of the physical body allows us to actually feel the ego as well as our astral and etheric bodies. The original content of the soul exists as the primary origin of that which is ultimately expressed, during incarnation, in the physical body. The consistent, concerted effort to stay conscious during the day erodes, and eventually destroys, that same body. When death finally arrives at long last, the Higher Hierarchies and the angels approach us to initiate a special process: the creation of energy and vigor for a new and fresh incarnation.

During life in the earthly realm, there exists in human consciousness a sacred triad comprised of thinking, feeling and willing. In both thinking and willing, the higher worlds can project themselves easily into earthly realm, helping us with actions we are unable to complete on our own; but in feeling, the incarnated soul is totally free and independent, even here on earth; "we are completely ourselves" here, and can make feeling based choices and decisions that are utterly our own. Feelings form a mirror image of all that exists just outside of our day-to-day consciousness, including realms in the beyond, and can also reflect and reveal our own divine spiritual essence. They help us to understand and perceive the heavenly realms, invisible to many, but available to all through intentional clairsentience and psychic sensitivity. Feelings lead the way to actual participation in the creative workings of the gods, and in this way, human beings are able to harness great spiritual power from the earthly realm. If we pray with feeling and open, vulnerable sincerity, we can effect healing for others, remove stress from our lives, and even save lives or prevent unhappiness, stress and discord in others. Our spiritual studies, therefore, should absolutely be accompanied by heartfelt feelings in order to bring about the greatest efficacy in prayer. It is our responsibility, as human beings, to the universe.

51

In our time, human beings are able to conceptualize the workings of the ego, even to the point of manipulation; but in past times, we did not yet have such a capacity, and as a result, our actions were less thought-out, less studied, less self-conscious. Unfortunately, egocentrism and misuse of the personality have now grown to such an extent that they can lead to tremendous problems, even on the global scale, including war, domination and control of basic goods and necessities. Many world leaders operate exclusively from the simplistic, greed-driven manifestation of the ego, and in the process, have created circumstances dangerous to the earth as well as to the physical and spiritual self. Both the freedom of the individual and the health of the populace as a whole are threatened. Gaia has been pushed to the point of potential non-recovery.

Modern philosophy, on the other hand, expresses a healthier understanding of the ego: it advises looking inward instead of outside of ourselves for answers, as was primarily done in earlier phases of human spiritual evolution. This includes avoidance of the habit of looking outside of ourselves for excessive approval, validation or celebrity. At the end of the day, people can only find inner peace with a full understanding of the inner workings of the ego, with a solid sense of how to calm and tame its negative aspects while still honoring that which is wild and free within all of us. It can be a stubborn, thorny process, but if we calm the ego sufficiently to receive the information we find by looking within, we can achieve true freedom and preserve our innate identity in all its splendid singularity. We can live a life of spiritual beauty and harmlessness with regard to others. Both the etheric and physical bodies are necessary for true ego consciousness, and the development of the ego is, as we have seen, made possible by the gradual destruction of our physical selves with each waking day. If we are spiritually healthy, the superficial needs of the ego lessen as earthly life progresses and as the body ages and weakens, just as surely as any known, irresistible force in the universe. This is a risk we take gladly, because when the soul has passed into the next realms, it begins to view physical aging as a privilege, an honor and a willing sacrifice.

If, at some point during physical life, we hurt someone we are meant to love, we then gravely diminish the value of our true ego, and experience painful emotions in the afterlife over our misdeed, actually feeling the full extent of it as if we were the other person. The soul, which may not have been able to feel the pain of the other while still in the earthly realm, now has the opportunity to do so through Christ consciousness. Conversely, as long as we remain in our ego -- on earth, in our physical body -- we have complete power to make amends to others. It is advisable to do so as soon as possible, without waiting, because we really never know when we might see the other person again. A heartfelt apology, with the soul laid bare in humility, is all it takes.

In the astral body, humans move and grow into the heavens as the soul expands after death. Here on earth, we can live out our karma and experience things differently in the "I" consciousness than we may be able to later, in the astral body. This is because our needs and views may then turn out to be quite the opposite of what they were in life. After death, both conscious and unconscious desires remain, with the latter becoming very strong. This sudden shift in perception is commonly caused by imbalance between the two modalities of consciousness during physical life. Subtle spiritual desires and passions, during life on earth, are sometimes kept deep within the very core of our being, and the ego can actually remain ignorant of them if heavily distracted by all of the insistent currents of daily life.

An "extract" of the astral and etheric body is taken through to the greater heavens after the soul's experience in Kamaloka, the first stage after death. The true, permanent "I", or ego, remains always unchanged; it is not like the "I" of earthly life, which is obliterated during sleep. In earthly life, we experience the "conceptive I"; in spiritual life, we experience the true "I", which is most able to be present when we are *not* here on earth. It is also the most important "I", because it is the "true ego". The true "I" is already active from birth, and it represents the active principle in learning to walk, speak and think. The spirits of form —the beings from which the human form originates -- are responsible for helping us along in these developmental areas in early incarnation.

Unfortunately, other spirits might try to cast us down just as we are learning and growing. They are not evolved spirits; they should have evolved to become spirits of motion, but instead have manifested as Luciferic spirits "consigning humans to gravity" in an attempt to prevent our own conscious awareness. It is important to pray for spiritual protection and to establish strong boundaries, especially around children, by praying to God and asking for the assistance of the angels in delivering the message.

Human beings enter quite gradually into the physical world. The "most perfect part", and the most developed at birth, is the head, and our consciousness emanates from it. To the clairvoyant, everyone's head radiates light and visible energy; the aura can be seen most strongly and brightly there. The ancient Atlanteans saw something similar: a shining vapor, a fire or a light over the heads of prominent thinkers. It is possible to teach oneself to notice the aura: try softening your gaze around a person who is standing in front of a white or beige wall. If you are a student, you have the perfect opportunity, because you may automatically notice the aura of your professor as you look at him or her standing in front of a relatively blank wall, during a lecture. See what colors you can notice.

The cycles of human physical life average seven years in length. From ages one through seven, awareness of the "I" gradually bursts forth, helped along by the incredible life force of the child, their capacity for curiosity and their innate, inborn passion for unlimited learning. The entire life experience at this age, compared with other developmental stages, is quite internal. Normal spiritual beings who have already gone through the cosmos and developed as powers of goodness, such as guardian angels and departed loved ones, can affect children in positive, strongly protective ways during this first cycle of life.

For the growing child, each cycle begins on the level of the physical and proceeds inwardly, affecting first the external, then the internal body. By the time of the second dentition, the apex of the first formative cycles in the life of a child has been reached. By age seven, "essential form has been given; the rest is only growth." Until that age, we have at our disposal great elasticity of form and thought. Backward (Luciferic) spirits can sometimes attempt to approach from the outside and "imprison...what is otherwise elastic." This can result in a dichotomy of evolutionary forces at odds with one another, and can produce a tightening, even a rigidifying of thought and form if left unattended over time.

Negative forces, because they act against normal cycles, manifest as quite irregular in their strength, and therefore do not possess the steady, quiet strength of positive forces. They need not be feared if divine protection has been requested through prayer. In fact, the energy of fear will only attract them. Work with yourself to find ways to calm the seductive forces of fear. Our culture has, perhaps unwittingly, promoted concepts of fear, submission and death very strongly, saturating our minds with images of terror and helplessness.

These pathways of thought need not be followed within the boundaries of your own mind, however. Turn off the television news, take a walk outside where you can be closer to the elemental spirits, and ask God, Jesus and the angels for assistance. Speak with

55

a friend or trusted counselor if need be. Free yourself.

CHAPTER V

Sleep and the Four Necessary Bodies

In sleep, we unconsciously slip into a realm quite similar to the afterworld. As our physical self remains relatively stationary, our soul travels, and bears witness to great and fantastic beauty. Even someone who is not sensitive or clairvoyant can experience awareness of this kind. In some ways, the sleeping state of humans (our physical and etheric bodies) can be compared with that of plants, while the moon represents our astral body and the sun, our ego. The sun and moon act upon plants just as the ego and astral body act upon the physical and etheric bodies of the sleeping person. "The whole cosmos is involved in the growth of plants," because the sun acts upon the height of the plant, and the moon acts upon its width. As dreamers, we lie still, bathing in the effects of our astral consciousness and true ego awareness. In this way, we are able to receive visions and sometimes visitations from those who have already passed into the sky world ahead of us.

Human beings are essentially "formed as an extract from the forces of the cosmos". Expressed in another way, our body, mind and spiritual awareness are steeped in all the surrounding heavenly influences, much like plants were steeped in the herbal tinctures of old tradition. Sunlight (the "I", or ego) has about it "a soul spiritual nature" in addition to its physically warming and brightening rays, and we absorb this as we live and breathe. The human astral body contains within it the light of the moon, with all of its spiritual wisdom. Therefore, the ego is an extract of solar influence, while the astral body manifests as an extract of lunar influence.

During sleep, the astral body and the ego travel far beyond the physical body, rising up to take on a greater, expansive, simultaneous, omniscient state of being. We know that we sleep in order to revive the energy lost to the activities of the day, and that a slightly higher level of exhaustion takes place each time due to the repeated crashing-in of the ego each morning, until a tipping point is reached and the physical body begins to weaken, leaning ever more toward death. Opposition to and destruction of the body caused by the inherent, repeated pattern of sleeping and waking is necessary for soul life. After death, from a different vantage point, it is considered to be a blessing, and we are grateful for this disintegration.

If it is true that we die gradually as we live, then excellent self-care, both emotionally and physically, should be followed to slow this process to a certain extent, removing years of unnecessary fatigue and wear originating from sources other than the sleep cycle. Find a fun workout that you enjoy reasonably well, commit to it, and watch your youthful energy begin to return within days. Reduce your stress level as much as you can by making the intentional choice to shut tension out of your life. Include as much organic, antioxidant-rich food as you can in your diet, and your body will reward you for the reduced toxin load by feeling far lighter and more agile. You will also be avoiding, to the greatest extent possible, the stratospheric amount of carcinogens now used in farming and sprayed directly onto our food. By supporting our physical and emotional selves, the repeated impact of daily awakening can be minimized effectively through the cultivation of good health, and we can better live out our life purpose, honoring divine intentions for our lives and connections here on earth.

At night, the ego and the astral body act to illumine us, to guide us. When we awaken, it is like the setting of the sun and the moon, and the end of our plant-like existence; these forces fall temporarily away as we break through to consciousness. Because we live consciously, vitality naturally dies in us over the course of waking life, but this can be assumed with great acceptance and dignity. The rhythm of falling asleep and waking up continues, on and on, day after day. After the occurrence of death, the ego and the astral body (the source of our consciousness during waking life) emerge as our sun and moon, but with nothing to illumine. In other words, our physical and etheric bodies have been shed, and we exist as pure consciousness. Previously established soul connection with Jesus and the Higher Hierarchies allows them to then illumine us with their spiritual light.

The physical, astral, etheric and egoic represent the four necessary bodies, acquired and destroyed over many incarnations, that allow us to experience further stages of development as human souls. Between death and a new birth, the soul is given a new astral, etheric and physical body; what was destroyed in the last lifetime is therefore repaired, created for us anew out of the macrocosm. The forces for repair of the four necessary bodies reside within the solar system and greater universe, and we must be able to receive them properly in order to move forward and into the next physical incarnation. After death, our being expands widely outward and into the universe, extending itself into the stars for full repair of astral body.

The human body acts as the most convenient possible means for soul expression, the most hospitable form for the deepest impulses and feelings of spirit. In many ways, we can still learn from the plants: they close when the sunlight fades, and reopen when its warmth arrives again the following day. In human beings, it is the ego and the astral body that come and go, in the regularity of sleeping and waking. Both of these "are born out of the space to which the Sun belongs, and do not belong to the earth at all." In sleep or in death, human beings leave the earth and join a larger world outside the physical realm. At these times, the ego and the astral body are totally independent and can go their own way, because our true home can be found in the sun and the planets, and we are comfortable and nourished there. Daily life -- that which we consider to be our full reality -- is, to the reality of the soul, actually more like sleeping. As human souls, we are only fully awake when we are in the great world, in a state of full liberation.

Our physical eyes and ears exist only because of adaptation to earthly conditions, and have evolved to help us here, in this realm. They are not, contrary to common opinion, the only means by which we can see and hear. Through direct occult vision, clairvoyants know that the ego and the astral body, both comprising the soul, belong to "the world of the stars", and that separate, sweeping faculties of perception exist in that realm. In our age, the soul and the body reside relatively far apart from one another, which was not the case in ancient times; humans were able to see outside of themselves, as a matter of course, events and visions originating in the spiritual realm. The human soul has since become more solitary and individual, less community-based; psychic and faith-based phenomena have become more rarified and, as a result, highly sought after by many seeking healing and enlightenment.

During sleep, the soul effectively leaves the physical body, as well as most of the etheric body, behind; quite literally, we leave our bodies lying in bed. Between death and rebirth, we are living in the "star world" and are related to the astral forces while existing in their realm, but we have no real consciousness of these places during sleep because we are not meant to witness such restorative powers during physical life. They are effectively hidden from us during this time, because it is not the right moment in our evolution to see them. Physical science of the body, however, comes no closer to encompassing a full knowledge of the human being. We are therefore left with Anthroposophy and religious and spiritual faith to navigate each successive heavenly realm at the proper time. In the meantime, we receive shining glimpses of alternate forms of awareness through our dreams.

We have established that while on earth, our sleep state is similar to the realms between death and rebirth; but our field of awareness during earthly sleep is an unconscious one, whereas awareness between death and rebirth is fully conscious. We know exactly what is happening, even if we are not able to influence all of the events and heal all of the relationships we may wish. If we happen to wake up in the astral body during sleep, however, we are in a state that is the exactly same as that between death and rebirth, with full clairvoyant consciousness.

Sleep, in our culture, is usually viewed quite simplistically. The quality of rest derived from a nap, for example, differs subtly from nighttime sleep, and this variation is readily apparent to everyone. During sleep, however, the "I" aura (not the astral aura) does something more, of which people are not commonly aware: it energetically divides the body, at the throat, into two parts. The lower part is darker; and healing, restorative forces emanate from it. The upper part shines as brilliant rays moving outward into the universe, absorbing the forces of "the world of the stars". This higher aura, visible in full color to clairvoyants and sensitives, develops "forces of attraction from the star world" for the purpose of rejuvenation during sleep.

In Steiner's time, as a "natural course of evolution", people were rapidly losing awareness and knowledge of the heavens, even letting go of scholarly information with regard to the constellations and moon phases. In past times, of course, people experienced greater knowledge of the heavens; they were individually and collectively affected by "all of the astral forces in space". Before scientific or logical thought, the ancient ones lived more by instinctive action; the movements of the constellations were actually felt as a full-body experience for them, and they received spiritual information in a direct manner, from space. Today, people commonly use only their physical sight to view the panorama of the stars. The artwork created by the ancients to depict the heavens and the constellations actually represented what they saw, and each image, for them, showed a powerful, real and gigantic spiritual being, not just a dot-to-dot outline of an earthly creature. With the passage of the Pleiades overhead, for example, people commonly turned inward in self-reflection as a group. The waking life of the ancients, in those days, resembled far more closely the spiritual world between death and rebirth. Events in space acted upon the sensitive human astral body, and caused massive shifts within the psyche. Today, these changes are no longer so readily perceived. There has been a weakening of the human ability to directly perceive transmissions from the heavens.

In antiquity, there was no need to prove the existence of life after death or the immortality of the soul, because people could already clearly see and perceive these phenomena through direct psychic knowledge. In the early Egypto-Chaldean age, people experienced during earthly life what is now experienced between death and rebirth, in the planets. By the Greco-Latin age, only a remembrance of these abilities remained; they had already been largely replaced by the logic and judgment born into that era. Aristotle made reference to the "sphere spirits", because these powers had not yet withdrawn deeply into the soul, and could still be perceived by a few. Gradually, humans lost awareness of the spirit beings in both waking and dream life. Today, we are sometimes able to access a shadow of an ancient memory if something "pierces through" our consciousness in just the right way, but we might only know that it was significant, and remain unable to remember the details. Starting in 1604, an active suppression of ancient memory came to us from a certain constellation of the stars. We still have these abilities, in the depths of our souls—just not directly, because the powers have withdrawn deep within.

In sleep, the upward aura still perceives information from the heavens, but not consciously. Anthroposophy allows this ability to be rediscovered, because it uncovers long-buried information deep within the soul, and awakens us sufficiently to access ideas long forgotten. After death, through spiritual science, we can still develop the awareness of the ancients as far as the Venus sphere, but we must have deep soul preparation in order to do the same for the Sun sphere. This awareness of what is necessary acts as strong illumination for the afterlife; for if we find ourselves disdainful of life here, our way will not be adequately lit after death. The "soma juice" of ancient times "will flow again from these individual souls" who have brought Anthroposophy through into the modern age.

What we view here on earth as mere concepts and ideas become *living forces* after death, but this only applies to our inner consciousness, because that is the core of our total perception after death. Awareness during life can feel intensely invigorating, and not just consciously; we may not even know that we are experiencing it due to the somewhat myopic focus the physical world brings. After death, we see everything broadly and directly. We are required to receive all-encompassing teachings that help us to grow and progress toward with the ultimate spiritual evolution of humanity. Steiner predicted that people in the future -- and that might be now -- would no longer have enough of the natural life-giving forces, and would experience premature aging; he also thought that a "decadence of physical humanity" would come to pass. We have only to look inside of a contemporary fashion magazine to see that he predicted correctly.

During physical life, being shut off from the greater universe is necessary, because it allows fresh awareness to be reborn once again onto the earth through the process of reincarnation. Ordinary, earthly thoughts and perceptions lack the deepest mysteries and secrets of existence, which cannot be found outside of us; they must be found within, at the core, soul level. Our psychic vision and ability to experience spiritual awakening during sleep is hidden, on earth, from most people, as well as from everyday observation. If we are able to see divine beings around us, it means that the ancient "thoughts of the gods...have been preserved." We are tapping into the genetic memory of our ancestors, and receiving a flash of what it felt like to live life as one of them. Maybe we still know, after all. It is certainly still possible to become clairvoyant, both during waking life and during sleep, even if one has never experienced episodes of psychic ability before. It is encoded within all of us. It is important to listen to our gut feelings, to honor them, and to remain open.

CHAPTER VI

Kamaloka and Karma

The world after death is just as real as this one, and in all stages except Kamaloka -- the first, intermediary stage after physical death -- the afterlife acts as a separate, profound, sometimes lengthy initiation for the human soul. We must pass through Kamaloka first. This new reality for the recently deceased soul extends as far as the outer orbit of the moon. There, connections with others are as real as those experienced during life -- and they are also with the same people we knew on earth. There exists in Kamaloka a distinct heaviness placed upon the soul, and it is caused by our newfound inability to further a connection with another previously known in physical life. In early Kamaloka, we have within our awareness only the experiences the soul has received on earth. This gradually changes as we adjust to both the afterlife and the presence of the Higher Hierarchies, or angels,who shine upon us and encircle us with spectacular light of many astral colors. The introduction of the light of the angels thus begins, little by little, to erase our consciousness of earthly life as we move gradually away from preoccupation with the earthly realm. During Kamaloka, we still experience with full force all of the pressing concerns of physical life, even though we now live entirely cut off from it.

During earthly life, we need moral consciousness to create a harmonious experience. In Kamaloka, the intentional goodness with which we have lived our physical lives keeps our soul visible to the Hierarchies, so that they may find us and shine upon us, and so we may discern that which is around us and become properly oriented in that realm. Immoral consciousness, on the other hand, is dimmed even further in Kamaloka; the surroundings of such a soul become completely darkened, and all consciousness is replaced by a state of fear.

Right after death, we can have connections with those we knew on earth, in addition to those already in the afterlife who died at around the same time we did. From earth, living human beings can convey thoughts to the departed while holding a vivid image of them, and those of us still on earth must be generous with this. In this way, friendships continue. We see our ancestors, but this lasts only for a short time. At first, after death, one sees one's own life and recalls the relationships one had on earth. The urge is to look down upon the earth. Souls are conscious of the fact that they must eventually return to earth, if they somehow lost consciousness of the existence of earth, they would also lose consciousness of their own ego, and would therefore lose all awareness of their own existence. It is not possible for the earth to completely disappear in the eyes of the departed, yet neither must they remain fixated upon it as their only source of reality.

During this first stage, those still on earth can connect with souls in Kamaloka most easily if the departed souls also reach out to them with their thoughts -- just so long as their consciousness during life has been pure and well-intentioned. Right after death, it is totally impossible for the soul to make new connections; one is limited to the established ones from the physical world. Nor can the dead find new connections who can teach them further in spiritual matters, after death; they can only meet individuals they have known while living on earth. All that can be seen by the dead is purely spiritual knowledge and feeling, because the five senses are no longer active. Everything is perceived through psychic visions. After death, souls often have only a dim perception of one another; but if they have acted as a beacon of spiritual love before passing through the gate of death, they can do the same after crossing. Such souls can perceive those around them with clarity, extending awareness across the opening between the worlds and reaching out successfully to those left behind.

During our time in Kamaloka, we are still, quite naturally, longing to be connected with the earth. Visions of our loved ones and others we knew pull our attention back to everything that happened there, with great insistence. The collection of remembrances and souvenirs we hold in our consciousness reflects with perfect accuracy the way in which we chose to spend our life on earth. We are still highly preoccupied with the realm of memory, and find ourselves bound up almost entirely with the concerns and events of the physical world, which reach even into the immediacy of the present moment. A soul therefore lives, albeit temporarily, within the self-made construct of everything that they have experienced on earth.

The function of Kamaloka is to set aside earthly interests, which cannot, in any case, be satisfied after death and must be removed as a point of overriding concern. Kamaloka follows a "brief, embryonic period of sleep". During Kamaloka, we may not see every single person, now also deceased, we knew on earth; but the fact remains that we do come into contact with the people we were closest to. We are related to them in Kamaloka in exactly the same way we were related to them on earth, but now, as we have seen, nothing at all about the relationships can be changed beyond the point of death. We are spiritually bound to a relationship as it manifested on earth, but we are not limited only to the traumatic or the painful; we gain an awareness and vision of the whole, as it was lived out. Any wish left unmet, in this context, takes on great importance and focus. Desires we may have concealed during life will become more active after physical death, elucidating the nature of the true self. Equally, certain elements of the afterlife can influence the astral body and soul life of those left on the physical plane, causing the departed to lean, after death, toward people or concepts they may have been wholly indifferent to while on earth. Even after Kamaloka, this type of focus on and interest in the astral element as embodied on earth can still persist, but this must also be left behind over time.

In Kamaloka, the spatial proximity of souls does not automatically equal togetherness -- the kind we automatically think of when picturing a group of people standing in the same room, for example, as they would on the earthly realm. The soul has already expanded, is permeable, and can actually occupy the same space as other souls. Two or more souls thus taking up the same space can actually be quite psychically distant, one perhaps not even aware of the presence of the other; and their ability to connect is now completely dependent upon the spiritual purity of their relationship as well as the inner, moral state of each individual soul.

At the end of Kamaloka, we are compelled to leave behind desires and emotions related to earthly life; these then become permanently inscribed in the Moon sphere, and are recorded there in the form of an "account of debts" owed by every soul who has ever passed through Kamaloka, where human beings come to terms with who they are on the soul level.

Thoughts that used to belong to the inner realm of consciousness appear externally in Kamaloka as a "mighty panorama" spread before us in the spirit world. After death, one's inner self begins the process of causing the content held within the soul to grow, change and evolve to a higher level. The spiritual pain of the dead is actually self-induced, formed and created according to choices freely made during physical life, and such feelings are experienced much like the dull persistence of a headache. The state of the soul in Kamaloka, whether painful or peaceful, arises directly from the way of life one has followed on earth. We suffer, after death, every last bit of distress we have previously inflicted upon others. We feel their pain exactly as if it were our own, and "a moral injustice can hurt" in the same way that physical pain causes searing trauma in the earthly realm. We bring it all, it seems, upon ourselves; but "to know karma alleviates the pain," and proper preparation, in the form of kindness, can ease or erase any potential suffering. Without knowledge specific to the workings of karma, however, humanity will run into serious impediments to its proper and intended evolution.

To extinguish oneself on earth in an act of suicide can lead to a phase of loneliness and a feeling of entrapment in Kamaloka. The soul can feel encased and tightly confined, at least temporarily, within a gray cloud, burdened with an immense sense of pain and frustration at the course of events surrounding their death. They may remain unable, for a time, to communicate with dear ones left behind. Reading to the dead, as described in the chapter on Anthroposophy, can help with their release toward further spiritual evolution in Devachan, the heavenly plane and true afterlife.

Such a soul can sometimes be reached by psychically sensitive family members who continue to be impacted by the pain of their loss. A healthy spiritual life here on earth, including immense peace and forgiveness directed toward the self, ultimately increases the chances of communication with all other souls in both directions between the worlds, and enhances the ability of each soul to move forward after death in a state of comfort. If a family member or friend has taken their own life, please allow yourself time to integrate the enormity and shock of your loss, and find trusted support systems to assist you in the process. Take exquisite care of yourself, and understand that you are not to blame. Suicide brings about a particularly sharp type of pain, and time for healing must be allowed, with compassion expressed toward the self and the departed one. Souls who have passed in this manner can eventually find a beautiful kind of healing through the practice of reading to the dead. Those left behind on earth actually have more influence on a soul in Kamaloka than they can have upon themselves. They also have more influence on the departed one than other deceased souls can possibly exert. People still living in the physical realm can "bring about changes in the departed", all in the direction of ease, peace and healing.

Between death and rebirth, there is no inherent light at all. Without the light of the angels and heavenly beings, the afterlife is like the night sky without the stars. We must have already kindled spiritual light on earth, especially through close connection with the golden light of Jesus, and successfully taken His love with us through the gate of death in order to psychically see in the afterlife. While in the spiritual realm, remembrances of life in the physical realm can only be perceived through psychic visions. In time, after Kamaloka, the soul finds it increasingly difficult to remember, and forgetting sets in.

At first, in Kamaloka, relationships exist at the emotional and spiritual level they achieved during life, in the very same state they were in when one of the participants died. As we have noted, if there was a relationship in which we were intentionally unkind, we are sentenced to witness, again and again, exactly the discomfort we caused the other person to feel in physical life; and we must view it for a length of time perfectly equal to the actual earthly event. We actually feel it, very intensely, just as the other person did. From this vantage point, we are unable to make good because of the unchangeable nature of the realm of Kamaloka. We must experience, in full force, the very same pain we gave to others. We can perceive the wrong very well, but cannot in any way alter it. Through this spiritually demanding lesson, we attain the awareness and knowledge of exactly how our treatment and consideration of another must be changed and made better within the frame of the next life. We have the power to change and transform karma when re-entering the physical realm, and this represents our chance for forgiveness and absolution in the eyes of the divine.

In this first phase after death, we are gradually growing away from physical life. We still feel the same feelings we felt on earth, and experience the interpersonal connections we had during our physical lifetime. A sense of intense deprivation is common, because the soul is still longing for the physical body and relationships so recently

70

left behind.

The sphere of Kamaloka reaches all the way between earth and the outer orbit of the moon, but the types of experiences mentioned above usually take place while the soul is still hovering quite close to earth. Souls can be kept closer to the physical realm because of their own wishes, unmet goals or passions, or a sudden, untimely death. They can also remain bound because of unresolved connections and relationships, pain upon leaving others, or the fact that they are still used to living in a human body and find it hard to readjust to the spirit world. Narcissistic or materialistic people have a harder time with this;the first stages of Kamaloka create in them an "emotional disturbance in the astral body" because during life, they were entirely dependent upon others for positive reinforcement, and did not understand the value of building inner reserves for spiritual self-validation.

Most of the souls that mediums can connect with from here are still somehow bound to, or hovering over, the earth. Still another reason for their remaining could involve a state of anxiety for those left behind, especially friends and family. This results in a type of self-created, magnetizing effect that keeps souls close to their earthly home. It is important to pay attention to the prevalence of this problem so that we can help the dead. The living can help relieve anxiety, for example, by providing or fulfilling a need for a child left behind, if that was the source of worry, in an act of selflessness and devotion. Sometimes, the deceased person can feel condemned to their fate, and this can be a burden to the clairvoyant until a key situation on earth is ameliorated, thereby releasing its hold upon the departed. By carrying out actions of love and service on behalf of the deceased, we can help them to move forward. If they had definite plans they were unable to complete, we can assist in an honest attempt to finish their work in their place.

Eventually, the soul grows beyond Kamaloka. The dead are by no means confined to one place at any given point; we have established that the "whole soul being is expanding" after death, moving out through the successive planetary spheres. From the Moon sphere, the soul grows even larger and begins to cross into the enormity of the next sphere. In the afterlife, the dead find that they are never actually separate from one another, as physical beings are on earth; they are instead "spatially intermingled", though they may not be consciously aware of this fact. They are fully capable of sharing the same space without knowledge that the other is there. In other words, the soul is not actually isolated; it can occupy the same space as an infinite number of other souls.

In the Moon sphere, all of our imperfections have been inscribed into the Akashic Chronicle, where there exist all of the recorded successes, failures and facts about the astral body, including trivial details. Non-fulfillment of life purpose is also inscribed, and the soul adds these lessons to its Kamaloka experiences, usually finding that life intentions that have been simply but unintentionally unfulfilled are not serious affronts to our karma. This is why the clairvoyant can best see imperfections in the soul between the Earth and the Moon. After the Moon sphere, the soul begins the Devachanic, or heavenly, experience.

The rules are not known exactly or in minute detail, but in general, good moral composition of the soul here on earth allows us to reliably exist as social beings in Kamaloka and in higher realms. With traits of goodness as our spiritual foundation, we are able to connect with other souls, and also with the angels and higher beings. Defective moral constitution of the soul, on the other hand, allows us only to be solitary spirits in the next worlds, able to readily see others and to cry out to them, but unable to be seen or perceived ourselves.

The end of Kamaloka is the most important time for the clairvoyant attempting to reach out to the departed soul, for whom this new, transitory period is initially experienced as yet another "violent shock", quite comparable in feeling to the earlier, earthly death. In actuality, passing out of Kamaloka brings about quite the opposite: the finite, physical life leads directly to the higher realm of Devachan and, ultimately, to resurrection and rebirth here on earth.

CHAPTER VII

Devachan and the Heavenly Spheres

After Kamaloka, the soul expands further into the universe, and we travel into the stars for restoration of the astral body. While in the greater spiritual world, called Devachan, we grow into cosmic space, our soul taking the shape of the enormous planetary spheres, ever widening as we progress. We proceed from one planetary orbit to the next, effectively growing into the macrocosm. With each stage, very specific lessons are learned, and with each stop along the way, we advance as far as the edge of that particular planetary orbit. Individuals holding different morality sets attain differing degrees of soul advancement on the journey between physical lives. The realm of Devachan encompasses all of the happenings of the true afterlife within the spheres of our planetary system and beyond.

Departed souls float into celestial reality and become one with the heavenly worlds. They cumulatively take up greater amounts of space in the universe, and the way in which they experience the journey is dictated by the quality, composition and honesty of the individual, ethical being. The earthly morality learned and held precious by the soul during physical life prepares us for living in the next world as spirits capable of communication with others and with the Higher Hierarchies.

In Devachan, we find ourselves compelled to psychically bring our wishes to us, instead of simply going to them, as we do in the physical world. Everything presents itself to us according to the state of the soul upon the moment of entry into Devachan. A laying down of the proper foundation is essential, and this preparation can only be accomplished during physical life. As in instances of earthly initiation, we may learn about ourselves through visions in the spiritual world. In physical life, perceptions arrived through the senses; after death, they arrive through visions. Everything we experience inwardly transforms itself into our objective outer reality, and we see outwardly exactly what we are inwardly. Nothing more is hidden or unconscious. Life after death shows us a true, completely honest and accurate reflection of ourselves.

Three major phases after death unfold as we travel through Devachan. First, we feel the full effects of our moral principles as we exercised them during earthly life; second, we experience the consequences of the religious beliefs we held during earthly life; and third, we understand that the soul would be utterly dimmed without the light of Christ and the Mystery of Golgotha.

Before Christianity, people could retain memory between lifetimes, but only because of initiation into knowledge dating back to the beginning of the earth. Now, these early traditions have faded away, and we must have an understanding of the mystery of Golgotha in order to remember our past lives. As we have seen, by the time of the Greeks, original knowledge from the beginning of humankind was already quite exhausted; they saw darkness, expressed as the Shades, after death. According to Homer, this was "the land of the Shades, where nothing can change."

With the mystery of Golgotha, people are now able to receive the light of Christ, which illumines our souls with His brilliant golden light, both on earth and during the middle period, or Sun sphere, in the phase between death and rebirth. Ancient spiritual knowledge can now be restored, but in a new way. The mystery of Golgotha was needed because of the declining spiritual state of humanity at the time of its occurrence and, in light of lost primeval knowledge, is still absolutely essential to humankind today. In Devachan, gorgeous "astral color phenomena" and shining, heavenly beings come to meet and surround the human soul, showing us the way to the first stop along the ascension of our spiritual growth in the afterlife.

After the Moon phase of Kamaloka, we move on to the planet **Mercury** (which is Venus in modern astrology). Mercury, for anthroposophical purposes, is considered to be the occult name of Venus, and for each of the planets mentioned, it is the spiritual entity that concerns us, not that actual, physical planet. From this sphere forward, the relationships we experienced while living in the earthly plane are absolutely cemented, frozen in time. We live in the Mercury sphere for a little while, and begin to inhabit wider cosmic space; we are no longer enclosed by the relatively small space of Kamaloka, but now expand to the wider sphere of the orbit of Mercury. We limit ourselves to those individuals we knew on earth, and with the exception of the higher beings, will continue to do so throughout Devachan. This is the sphere in which our earthly morality is shown in the harshest light, greatly impacting our abilities, perceptions, experiences, awareness and ability to connect with others. Souls devoid of morality find themselves increasingly helpless to locate their loved ones, because the limitation and grief they experienced in Kamaloka has only intensified and become more fixed.

In the Mercury sphere, we feel a strong impulse toward the development of our will, because we are beginning to better understand the real workings of karma. We can suddenly see everything with absolute clarity, and we know what we want to do differently next time. The Mercury sphere is the realm of unkept promises. This is where we deal with such inconsistencies, and learn how to elevate our souls in that regard. The realm of unfulfilled resolutions has already been experienced by the departed soul, on the Moon. In both cases, simple human imperfections, whether developmental or otherwise, are not considered to be terribly limiting and do not represent a significant threat to the peace of the soul. They can actually be of great value and significance, because they offer clear opportunities for further growth.

Mercury represents the moral sphere of karmic consciousness. Whether our existence there will be that of a social being or that of an isolated soul depends entirely upon the earthly life we have lived, which also determines the level of our ability to communicate and maintain relationships with the Higher Hierarchies.

As the soul progresses on to the sphere of **Venus**, we move from a focus on morality to a focus upon the religiosity we expressed on earth, and we feel the results according to its nature and extent. In this realm, we experience a lack of earthly religious inclination as a state of absolute discomfort and sharp pain. Souls join one another according to the religious or philosophical beliefs they held in physical life, and according to their earthly worldview and conception. No common religious consciousness exists on Venus; in general, people live separately according to personal experiences of the religion they followed while on earth. Neither is there division of the races here -- just soul experience and religious experience relative to the conceptions we held while living in the physical realm. The soul is "taken up into one of the great religious communities" of the afterlife. Materialists still live alone, caught in the cages of their earthly mental constructs.

Soon, the Higher Hierarchies approach us in the Venus sphere, as well, and begin to take us through the enlightenment of that particular phase of Devachan, shining a light upon our innermost religious soul nature and inherently personal belief systems. In the Venus sphere, those who were utterly opposed to religion in life fare the worst, as they experience a sense of enclosure and entrapment within themselves. Errors and mistakes made on earth become factual realities in the spiritual world. Thoughts freeze in place, preserved just as they were at the moment of physical death, and appear directly in front of us for examination. We cannot move or alter them while living outside the physical body in Devachan. All things in the spiritual realm are fixed and unchangeable.

After Venus, we expand upward into the **Sun** sphere, which exists as the middle point between death and rebirth. Our memories of earthly life have, at this juncture, almost completely fallen away. We draw ever further from physical existence and toward the brilliant luminosity of the Sun, where we find a new and temporary home. Here, just as in other spheres, we must be able to make connections with other souls so that we can move through the afterlife in a state of equality. In addition, and most importantly on the Sun, we must find ourselves capable of fully understanding *all* souls and *all* religions; otherwise, we will experience a sort of spiritual agony. Our understanding of the religions of others, like all else, must first have been established in the earthly realm, previous to our arrival in Devachan; and it must be sweeping, whole and complete. On the Sun, we encounter existence created according to our earthly understanding of every single worldly religion and, in effect, "all that is human." We may find our experience empty or filled, depending upon the way in which we lived our earthly life. We require a previously-developed faculty and solid perceptual foundation in order to adequately understand the spiritual world.

According to Anthroposophy, Christ is "a sun being" who originally traveled to earth from the sphere of the Sun. Human souls arriving at the Sun sphere with full consciousness of Him therefore live in the pure light of Christ, because this was his original home. As we connect to this sphere, we become habituated to it, and become Sun beings ourselves, for a time. If we understand the mystery of Golgotha, the anthroposophical reference point for all religion on earth, we easily understand the soul nature of other spirits living upon the Sun, specifically Christ, its ruling spirit. We come to know the sun spirits; they illumine us, and we are radiant with their light as it moves through and around us. Christ fills us with purity, beauty, spiritual love and forgiveness. As in the Grail saga, the Sun spirit can, in fact, be retrieved; as travelers through Devachan, we find Him again on the Sun. At all phases beyond the

Moon sphere, the soul exists as an aura of pure spirit, and its willingness and permeability facilitates the transmission of this love.

We also find, on the Sun, that Christ and Lucifer are brothers; and, shockingly, that Lucifer also holds a place in the spiritual realm, though he appears in a form far less harmful and dangerous than he does on earth. Here, he is an imperfect being who appears his original form as the brother of Christ. Jesus guides us fully through the Sun sphere, and we are in His hands. If we have prepared carefully for this moment, we find ourselves able to recall past unification with the Christ impulse while living on earth. On the Sun, just as in the physical realm, we must align ourselves very closely and carefully with Christ, and unite fully with Him in His light; we will then be able to remember our previous life on earth once we have passed, and successfully carry over lessons through the Sun sphere and into the next life.

A few souls, who chose a malevolent nature while living on earth or were careless and uneducated in the ways of Christ, may mistake one brother for the other in the Sun sphere, and begin to follow the negative aspect of Lucifer. When distinguishing between Jesus and Lucifer in the Sun sphere, it is not just the content of the words spoken that is important; the context and true meaning is most crucial. We must listen for this with deep faith and attention. This is the moment of crisis or salvation, the "deep cosmic mystery", the reason for all of our spiritual preparation on earth. It is only possible to distinguish between Christ and Lucifer, at this phase, through Anthroposophy. We must also have acquired on earth an understanding of who Lucifer is, because it is his role, as the brother of Christ, to lead us from the Sun and into the next spheres. This represents a huge challenge and test for the soul. With the Sun now below us, we must "hold fast in memory" to the Christ impulse so that Lucifer does not become a threat. The more we have received Christ in life, the stronger we will be as we travel through Devachan, tested along the way by a series of formidable obstacles.

In the Sun sphere, we try our best to live on the path of goodness, spiritual love and acceptance. "All differentiation between souls ceases," but the soul can still be conscious of a deep-seated loneliness if no understanding exists of the actual reasons for entering this realm.

Christ, before coming to earth, used to live on the Sun, and had a throne there; but when He was called, He left His home and came to earth with powerful and urgently needed spiritual purpose. He washed His magnificent light over the earthly realm. For this reason, we must experience Christ while we, too, live on earth; otherwise, we will find an "unintelligible entry" in the Akashic Chronicle in the Sun sphere. The root of Akashic is *akasha*, which means "primordial spatial substance"; and the information recorded in these records represents the deepest, most sacred soul contents and karmic decisions held within each of us.

The Christ impulse stands at the epicenter of human consciousness and evolution. The mystery of Golgotha occurred intentionally, at the essential time, and at the exact moment when humanity had reached a low point in its advancement. From that point on, an ascension of human spiritual awareness began to take hold; Humanity experienced a large-scale karmic rescue, put into motion by Christ, so that we could continue upon our assigned spiritual path toward goodness and light. Jesus gave us the means with which to access connection with Him from our spiritual core, no matter where on earth or in the universe we happen to be at any given time. He is always available to us if we have spiritually internalized His essence and message.

After leaving the Sun, the soul meets the original Lucifer in the **Mars** sphere, and we see the side that is now harmless to us, just so long as we hold strongly within our souls the light of Christ. He communicates to us all of the necessary information from outside of the earth and related spheres. On Mars, above the Sun, we recognize Lucifer "...as he was before he became Lucifer, while he was still a brother of Christ." Lucifer changed because he "remained behind...and severed himself from...cosmic progress," but "his harmful influence does not extend beyond the Sun's sphere." Above the level of the Sun, he exists as he was before. In the Mars sphere, we are "led by Christ, (and) rightly received by Lucifer." To get to this point in Devachan, we have to recognize and circumvent the second throne beside Christ in the Sun: that of Lucifer.

In the Mars sphere, sounds become more pronounced and meaningful, while visions hold less significance, allowing us to experience the true harmony of the spheres -- the world of sounds at the center of the universe.

Conditions on Mars are now quite different from how they used to be.

In theory, the realm was warlike in past times, before the 17th century as we perceive it in earthly time. Souls constantly battled one another there, and often carried the negative consequences of these actions with them far into the future, affecting and tainting the continued development of their personal karma.

Popular stories and conceptions about Martians and life on Mars are, as we now know through the advancement of space technology, completely baseless. The spiritual aspects of this realm are, in fact, the realities most important to Anthroposophy. It is not the actual planet or planets to which we refer, but to their spiritual realms and existence. On Mars, we are actually like ghosts, or aliens, to other spirits inhabiting this sphere. Likewise, "beings who are utterly foreign to the earth" can also pass through the Earth sphere, but only initiates are able to encounter them. On Mars, we are "itinerants", and so are the dwellers of other planetary spheres who pass through the sphere alongside us.

Buddha played an important role in the transformation of Mars from a warlike place to peaceful realm. He was spiritually present at the time of Christ's birth, and thus became aligned with Jesus. Buddha was spiritually assigned to bring healing to this realm, and became for Mars what Christ has become for the Earth: a saving grace, a force of peace, a light of guidance and love.

The mystery of Golgotha, in 33 A.D., began a time of spiritual ascent for everyone living within the earth sphere. Prior to this date, humans on earth had been in decline on all levels. Other planets also have their own, separate courses of evolution to follow, and inhabitants there must experience such journeys of redemption, as well. Mars experienced its own ascent through Buddha, who withdrew from earthly existence to become the redeemer and savior of that occult planet, in order to "inculcate peace and harmony" there. This was not so much a death for Buddha as a type of crucifixion and transference of his essential self to an alien, aggressive place. At the time of the earthly death of Buddha on October 13, 483 B.C., "a breath of peace" emanated from him. Both Earth and Mars processes still require a great amount of time to accomplish and resolve, allowing ample chance for success, elevation and ascension.

When passing through the Mars sphere, then, every human being has the chance to become a Buddhist or a Franciscan (Buddha was reincarnated as St. Francis of Assisi) and to experience all of the feelings of associated with these paths. This is of monumental importance for the souls of all human beings, as it gives us the chance to learn from a separate ascended master who is spiritually aligned with Jesus.

Continuing through Devachan, the soul then moves on to **Jupiter**. Once we have arrived at this sphere, our connection with the earth has become empty of meaning, and cosmic influences reign over our souls and psyches. The harmony of the Spheres changes in nature between Mars and Jupiter; it transforms, using a comparison we can understand from our experience in the earthly realm, from orchestral music to choral music.

On **Saturn,** we again face the moral existence we lived out on earth, and realize that we were not truly connected before, when we lived in our physical bodies. Our earthly life appears spread before us; everything is viewed on the level of true feeling and from the cosmic viewpoint. The soul experiences a "spiritual mirror image in reverse." While traveling through the cosmos, we cannot see or experience earthly events that occur between physical lives; we have become disconnected, and have no idea of what has happened on earth in the interim. In the Saturn sphere, however, all of the necessary spiritual knowledge is given, and we gain perspective and understanding that will help us to reincarnate. We gather new energy. "Spiritual forces stream from the cosmos" and wash through us, preparing us and refreshing us for a renewed birth.

The Saturn sphere is of special significance to the Anthroposophist because the energies we absorb there have to do with the natural human attraction to all that is purely spiritual. Assimilation of these lessons in the life of the soul can then be taken through to the next life. Each planetary sphere we pass through individually determines the faculties and impulses we will possess when we are reincarnated. The whole process builds upon itself, and the choices made by the soul engrave themselves into our karma more deeply with each successive life. After the Saturn sphere, we spread out into the greater universe and gather forces for our next incarnation. We bring all of the energies of the solar system, planets and outer cosmos with us into the next earthly existence.

In Devachan, we must become citizens of each of these places, in turn; we must find that we are able to make ourselves at home, for a time, in every sphere so that we can absorb the monumental nature and amount of knowledge offered, internalizing it into our core spiritual self.

As we travel, those still on earth will commonly reach out to us with their whole heart and soul. We have seen, when considering the state of Kamaloka, that they can reach us relatively easily if we also reach out to them with our thoughts. In Devachan, however, we are actually busy working on the "right shaping of (our) further karma." With our entire soul, we wish to return to earth so that we can live life afresh and correct our karma, and we *will* our karma to change in the period between death and rebirth. A child must relearn culture that has advanced since their last death, and so must start afresh in physical life. Culture on earth must have changed sufficiently while we were away in order to make this possible, and souls tend to wait until this has happened before re-entering the physical realm.

During the entire Devachanic experience, the soul is able to become aware of other souls who predeceased us in earthly life. In the spiritual realm, we live differently with the same people we knew on earth, according to the moral disposition we chose to bring with us through physical life. If a soul lacked morality during life, it cannot come together with family and friends in the spiritual world; a psychic shell or barrier of its own making prevents this. The soul becomes isolated, and actually begins to make holes in the universe while working on its own destruction. Souls with purified will, on the other hand, become "social spirits", finding connections with others in the heavenly realm. The religion one held on earth makes a dramatic difference, as well; it, too, determines whether we will become social or isolated in the spiritual world. Souls without religion feel themselves to be "enclosed, in a capsule or prison". Materialistic ideas held on earth "incarcerate us in the realm of the spirit", depriving us of the proper forces of attraction in the planetary spheres and, significantly, of the means by which to form and develop our future karma.

Knowledge, as it is gained in the sensory world, is vastly different from that acquired in Devachan. Everything there is reversed, and the experience is the heavenly opposite of the earthly one. On earth, everything comes physically to us, and we can also reach out ourselves, with our arms and hands, to draw something nearer or walk toward a desired object or location without a second thought. In the spiritual world, however, it is not possible to be active, or to draw anything to oneself as a matter of course, as we can here by stretching out our hand, for instance, to grab something. We must instead cultivate absolute calm of the soul center in order to allow things to happen *through* us. We wait patiently. It is a bit like being an artist in the physical world; we exercise immense, deep and reverent patience as our vision comes through and bursts into fruition on the canvas. There is no rush, no excessive agitation or excitement. In the spiritual world, we must create the mood, and draw that which we envision toward ourselves through our feeling. We must "wait for the moment of grace." "What we do here to act, we do in the spiritual world in order to know," and we must wait in stillness for what we desire to come to pass.

In the spiritual world, everything is visions; all is encompassed by them, and they are mirror images of physical reality. We are, quite literally, enveloped and surrounded by them. From death to rebirth, we live in an unchangeable world of visions, illumined by radiant divine beings as we ascend on our path through Devachan. The soul exists as a stream of visions illuminated by the light of the Higher Hierarchies.

In the spiritual world, the more still we are, "the less we strive" and the more inner silence we bring, the greater the knowledge and perception we can receive. The karmic patterning and information we bring from earth matters a great deal. Major sources of pain in the spiritual world are twofold, and can be defined in simple terms so that we may avoid their pitfalls. They come, firstly, from not having loved another enough, and secondly, from the realization that nothing in the spiritual world can fix what has been done (or not done) in physical life. It is impossible to make a direct adjustment in Devachan despite "full awareness that it ought to be different", and a great amount of spiritual suffering can manifest for souls who have not loved, on earth, according to the true longings of their higher selves. In the spiritual world, nothing can be altered in terms of "soul configuration"; the soul is, in effect, stuck with what it has brought through to the other side through the gate of death.

All of the cosmos, in Devachan, now streams into our being from all sides; "the firmament, after death, is filled with what we truly are in heart and mind," according to whether or not we have "received the mystery of Golgotha into our innermost soul". The full visual and karmic effect we receive in the heavenly realm is then brought down to the next life so that we may become more elevated human beings, better able to assist in the spiritual evolution of the earth. As the result of a successful journey through Devachan, we possess far stronger energy, soul content and will than we did when leaving the last life; "an all-around strengthening process" has occurred. In our next incarnation on earth, we are what the time between death and rebirth has made us.

In life, we live within the finite limits of our skin, but after death, we actually permeate everything, and live inside objects and things. One can discern similarities to many traditional cultures from the Anthroposophical viewpoint; consider, for example, the Native American religious view of nature, and the highly specific life force that pervades and emanates from every rock, tree, song, element and earthly event. Here again, spirit permeates the earthly world, to the great benefit of those in awareness.

By contrast, in an Estonian fire mythology, God taught the Estonians to listen in fire for language, but they only heard it according to their own particular love or distaste for any other group -- showing, in the end, the egoism inherent in their worldview. Christianity, as a source of relief, is devoid of egoism; if it is understood truly, it is completely selfless.

As we gaze into the night sky from earth, we see not only stars, but also our own characteristics recorded in the Akashic chronicle. This is the foundation of astrology, and the reason we love to look, with rapt attention and devotion, at the beauty of the night sky. Everything we transcribed into the stars during our time in Devachan unavoidably influences our next, reincarnated life, and the energy of the heavens can be felt quite strongly from the earthly plane. The starry heavens outside and the moral law inside each human being are, in truth, one and the same.

After passage into Devachan, the dead no longer actually use the language(s) they spoke in life; they instead send and receive thoughts, signs and visions, which encompass and bypass all language. Departed ones can understand physically-based earthly languages while still in Kamaloka, as transmitted through a message from a medium, for example.

After a number of years, a transformation comes about: their souls pass into Devachan,and we may lose touch with those who have died as they continue on their soul journey. All of their focus is required in order to build toward the next life.

Even as we mourn a departed loved one, we must remember that "the decay of the body has nothing to do with life after death." Human beings develop our souls in Devachan in order to carry them over into future lives. Openness to the spiritual during physical life leads, of course, to far greater ease and a better, more fluid experience after death; but even souls who have made imperfect choices during life will have the chance to develop their karma, and live again. In the meantime, all departed souls are everywhere, all around us, because they have expanded to the point of dwelling within all that exists.

In the future -- which, in the anthroposophical sense, is now -- "mankind will learn to be independent of what is bound to the physical body." Anthroposophy will further expand in consciousness and change its form, and "more will depend on how things are said rather than on what is said." As we saw when examining the Sun sphere, context is everything, and this is the key to understanding. Starting now, our psychic sensibilities will become more accessible, natural and automatic, and we will find it quite normal to communicate with loved ones who have passed.

In Devachan, thoughts that on earth belonged only to the inner realm appear externally as a pantheon of visions, spread out across the entire spirit world. After death, what was formerly one's inner world evolves content within the soul, and there takes place a reversal, a flip in placement from inner to outer reality, to which the soul must adjust.

As we have seen, any spiritual pain of the dead in Devachan is wholly self-induced; we suffer, after death, exactly that which we have inflicted upon others. After death, "a moral injustice can hurt" just as badly as physical pain hurts us on the earthly plane. We bring our experience after death upon ourselves; unconsciously or consciously, we select it. If we can bring ourselves to an understanding of the workings of karma in time, we can prevent or soothe our own pain. Without this knowledge, human evolution itself could not continue upon the path divinely prescribed for us by God.

Some souls, after death, are forced to carry out unpleasant tasks for Arhiman, the spirit of obstacles, and must serve that negative being. This is because of how they lived on earth:with too much love of ease and comfort, too much holding onto the old and resistance to new, positive, potentially uncomfortable change. This is very widespread in today's world. After death, these souls become agents of "the slowing-down process — the fettering of souls to the powers of opposition and hindrance." A lack of conscience in life delivers the dead to become servants of evil souls after they have passed from the physical plane. Beneath every consequence lies a spiritual underpinning. A soul who has become a servant of an evil entity, or a spirit of disease and death, shows us exactly how humankind has degraded itself. In life, we can choose to receive the spiritual world and thereby animate our soul, or we can dull ourselves and refuse to perceive; it is our choice through free will. We cannot by any means allow our innate spiritual powers to weaken or fade — we must nourish them with care, otherwise we deface and obliterate ourselves in the next worlds.

When Arhimanic beings control condemned souls, it is because these individuals lacked a sense of what is right during earthly life and experienced a corresponding propensity toward excessive luxury. If these souls, while in bondage, begin to understand why they are now obligated to serve an evil entity, they know exactly what they will have to do differently in the next life in order to adjust their karma. If they remain ignorant of these facts, they will only experience the same karma, and progress will be postponed. Their servitude is, fortunately, temporary; and they will be reincarnated, but having progressed no further.

The dead have the ability to see and understand purely spiritual knowledge and feeling. After death, souls can often register only a dim perception of one another; but if they have spent their physical lives radiating love and goodness, they can do so afterwards, as well — and keep on, in this way, across the gate between the worlds.

Either the soul stumbles through darkness in the spiritual world, or spiritual treasures are illuminated by the Higher Hierarchies for us to see. Light is also brought from earth, through us, to illumine them; this is our spiritual responsibility, our side of the heavenly pact. The soul is prepared for the afterlife by the thoughts and feelings directed toward the supersensible world during life. It does, in fact, matter how we perceive heaven during earthly life; and we must think often of the divine in order to secure a place of peace in the next realms.

If people have dulled themselves against spiritual feeling in a previous life, they will be further unprepared and weakened in the next incarnation, unable to understand as much as they previously knew, and incapable of full participation in physical and spiritual reality.

Their soul content in early Devachan remains below the level it could otherwise have attained. In this case, a second aspect is given the chance to intervene: Lucifer, in his dangerous form. Gifts from the higher beings are now illumined by Lucifer's light, instead, and twisted strangely, appearing through a different lens shot through with negativity. It is now Lucifer that illuminates the higher world for this type of person, with an altered, contaminated light that indelibly modifies and degrades the special gifts of that realm. Entering into the next life, souls receiving this treatment are still capable of forming a body, but they are spiritually lacking on the inside, even if they are capable of functioning in the outer world. They can live a smugly intellectual and purely mental existence, but without empathy or feeling, a life like this is both inadequate and spiritually destructive. These souls cannot later receive properly from the Hierarchies because they have consciously refused spiritual awareness in earthly life.

It is possible to identify human beings in the earthly realm who have been negatively influenced, through their own choices, in other realms. One often meets people during earthly life, for example, who have great difficulty in thinking clearly and efficiently. These souls were guided previously by Arhiman in the spiritual world, and during earthly life as well, in an ever-increasing cycle of negativity. Their personality traits include a tendency to be emotionally heavy, dull and hypochondriacal, and they find it inconvenient to be connected with others. If they are religious, it is only through a sense of egoism, and they only think of high spirituality as functioning through themselves. This type of "egoistic mysticism" often covers for serious, underlying moral decay. Additionally, cyclical association with Arhiman results in increasingly "defective logic" during earthly life and attraction of undesirable forces in the next worlds.

Clairvoyant insight into negative realms can bring a feeling of horror to the clairvoyant, whose energy is severely drained by such a vision. The guidance from the heavens, though, remains filled with loving wisdom in such cases. The overall lesson is that there exists no light without darkness anywhere in the universe, and that we are best prepared if we know what to expect, and how to cleanse and shield our souls ahead of time.

Luckily, on the earthly plane, we can choose to associate ourselves instead with spirits who continually transmit forces of healing into the world. The human soul then gains permission to enter into partnership with the powers of spiritual beauty in the time between death and rebirth, helping to shower the earth with goodness and light in specific, multitudinous acts of kindness. Souls with full awareness of empathy have special tasks assigned to them between death and rebirth, involving therapeutic and healing influences, and can be of great assistance to other souls in any realm. The efficacy of these gifts is felt according to the nature of the accompanying forces sent along by the Higher Hierarchies.

A clairvoyant can perceive whether or not an earthly soul has previously acted as a servant to the higher beings, who send pure love and healing to the world. These souls receive "profound blessedness" for present and future incarnations, and experience great joy, beauty and peace in both worlds.

From Devachan, the soul can remember Kamaloka, which lasts for some time. In that realm, souls lives as if they are still in their previous life, because they do not yet have the impression that they have moved on from the earth. Then, an understanding of the energetic reversal that has occurred arrives quite swiftly, and one enters into Devachan.

One looks within at the totality of the self, at the essence of the divine within, to see that we actually have all of the universe inside ourselves, including the stars and the outer worlds — and that our inner world of thought can now be seen, in magnificent form, outside of our souls.

In the higher realms, we are continuously rebuilding toward the rebirth of the fourfold physical body. In the Saturn period, we develop the "I" consciousness; in the Sun period, we develop the etheric body; and in the Moon period, we develop the astral body. When we return to Earth, we again have the chance to develop the true ego. By the time we return to the physical world, we carry within us transmuted conditions in the form of invisible energies that can usually only be felt. When all is said and done, the totality of the physical self is only made visible by the earthly conditions themselves; the rest of us originates from the cosmos. Between death and rebirth, we witness the developing human body, a work of art that is, to us, even more magnificent than the heavens themselves. We feel bliss because we are witnessing what will be, what we have created, and the beauty that is promised us. We are aware that will use our physical body later, but for the moment, in Devachan, it appears to us as the deepest possible mystery.

What happens when the human soul first meets with the Higher Hierarchies between death and rebirth? We experience a peeling away of spiritual layers, a laying bare of the soul, the release of the physical body and therefore of one's own destiny. The Higher Hierarchies can pass by us in two possible ways: either we know them, and are able to receive them in understanding through sufficient earthly preparation, or they pass us by, leaving us in darkness, unable to see them or anything else. Simply going through the gate of death, without benefit of preparation, is not enough to gain the understanding that will dispel the darkness and terrible solitude that can sometimes occur in the next worlds.

Most of the important inscriptions having to do with the recording of our total karma are made within the Sun sphere in Devachan. Outside of that particular realm, the soul must become accustomed to other necessary soul lessons and remain open to receiving knowledge not always within our conscious control.

The journey in Devachan can extend even beyond the planetary spheres. When we are approached by the Higher Hierarchies, we experience an expansion of the soul body into a giant sphere concurrent in size with the planetary realm we are currently visiting. As we progress, the soul progressively increases in size until it is massive, extending even beyond the last planet, as the time nears for rebirth. Numerous spiritual contracts are made over the course of our time in Devachan; and finally, it is time for the "spirit seed", concentrated and distilled back down to appropriate physical density, to find parents for the next life, bringing back to earth everything it has lived through over the course of the time spent in the heavenly realm.

In Devachan, the strengths and imperfections of the human soul are inscribed according to aspects specific to the particular sphere of soul travel. In this way, our karma is readied, and everything connected with our lives is etched into the heavens so that we may continue to work in conjunction with one another and, ultimately, with ourselves. The positions of the planets, familiar to us both astronomically and astrologically, really do indicate that which is inscribed both in the Akashic records and in our souls, and with clairvoyant vision, we can witness our karma written across the sky. Our "moral inheritance" appears anew, within each life in turn, as a "stellar constellation in our karma".

In essence, we are not truly beings of the earth. We are star beings, born to earth for a just a short while in order to work through our karma and the nature of our connections with others. Planetary life in the spheres even determines our physical appearance in the next life; human form cannot actually be derived solely from the earth. Our form symbolizes our inheritance as "an image of the Cosmos". Interestingly, Anthroposophy views it as a sin to study *only* earthly science, because there is so much more to be understood in the larger picture. The physical sciences, just scratching the surface, can only begin to guess at the sum of creation.

Certain remarkable souls, even those who are not yet ascended masters, have been able, over the course of history, to bring significant spiritual advancement to all of humanity.

Leonardo da Vinci, for example, brought to the earthly realm a spirit of human universality, but his vast goals and intentions remained incomplete at the time of his death. Because of his monumental accomplishments, "a colossal amount was inscribed by him in the Moon sphere," and Leonardo was able to then work through the many souls who followed after him in physical life. Inscription of his imperfections into the heavens, then, proved to be a massive source of inspiration for souls in the epochs that followed.

From this, we learn that what has not been perfected during earthly life becomes the seed for the next divine evolutionary process. Imperfections are not to be feared, but welcomed and celebrated in the spirit of mass group-consciousness.

Imperfection among souls, then, can lead to an intense burst of creative activity at the beginning of the next evolutionary stream. "The greatest blessing for a subsequent period is the fruitful imperfection...of an earlier period." Perfection, on the other hand, brings about an end, a conclusion to a particular stream of cultural consciousness and productivity. It is important to remain tolerant of, and grateful for, imperfection. It is important to understand this with feeling, respect and dignity, and to use our powers during physical life, instead of squandering them. This applies only to imperfections inscribed because of inescapable limitation — not to those recorded due to laziness or unkindness.

If those who have remained behind in the earthly sphere have spiritual thoughts living within their souls, the dead will be able to see these thoughts and ideas from their perspective in Devachan. Even if we previously held no spiritual thoughts while living on earth,, once we have been introduced to them, our particular souls "lights up" for the dead, and they can see us, take note of our accomplishments and help us along the way. This is the reason for human striving for perfection, and the reason why sincere, hard-working human beings with a sense of spiritual awareness can be assisted from the heavenly realm with information that seems to be channeled, or sent directly from above.

Additionally, it is imperative for the dead that we carry thoughts about the spiritual world to sleep with us at night. The more we can bring spiritual thoughts through from the day sphere and into the night, the greater the service provided to those who have passed into the heavenly realm before us. This carrying of thoughts is the substance by which the dead live; and they must also have done the same during life themselves, otherwise an immensely empty space will be experienced after death. A lack of prayer before sleep had already become very widespread during Steiner's time. He felt that concepts acting intentionally against the spiritual world were increasingly on the rise, and that the lack of evening prayer was "robbing the dead of spiritual nourishment."

All that is bounded by earthly consciousness represents the smallest fragment of the total life of the soul. After death, however, we experience the soul's true depth, and naturally make changes in terms of our priorities, consciousness and awareness of all matters. For this reason, if someone on earth ends up connecting with the dead from the physical realm, the departed souls can sometimes seem quite different to us. This is because of the massive amount of transformation, and the wide universe of realization, that their souls are undergoing. After death, they are, quite literally, flying through the cosmos, and the signs they are able to send to us are sometimes characterized by a similarly broadened scope, rather than by minute detail, especially as they journey further and further out into Devachan. Signs may come as especially spectacular rainbows or sunsets traversing the entire sky, for example, signifying the enormity of the soul's current sphere; and the moment at which they arrive communicates to us the authenticity of the message.

The ultimate human spiritual responsibility rests in carrying the highest possible moral consciousness through to the next worlds. What we do in this regard affects everyone and everything; quite literally, the entirety of the universe. It is therefore our personal responsibility to raise the vibration of everything that is. This is no small task, and it explains why so many are inclined to goodness, after all, especially as we get older or find ourselves facing the end of our physical lives. The challenge lies in grasping a solid sense of morality when young. Proper guidance for children is, of course, essential, and Steiner has provided for us a beautiful educational legacy. To be considered moral, we have to acknowledge that we have a relationship with *all* human beings. After death, moral souls find connections with other moral souls, supplying support and company for one another in Devachan. In this, way, further goodness is spread over the earth and throughout the universe, all by working together with divinely-inspired intention. Our ultimate mission in the earthly realm is to establish relationships of spiritual beauty. Anthroposophy serves to bring people together to initiate these connections in preparation for the time beyond the physical. Relationships can then be carried over, strengthening our efficacy as freed human souls. All that we possess rests waiting within our connections; they are everything, especially to the departed soul.

In Devachan, a crucial point is reached when we realize we must understand all earthly religions; this is absolutely essential to the healthy constitution of the soul. A correct understanding of Christianity helps with the impulse to understand all faiths, and to see everything as one. On earth, groups of human souls often delude themselves into thinking that there can only be one way to view God. Imagine: they are willing to go to war and kill another because of the way in which they view the totality of universal love! This, clearly, is illusion. Acceptance and spiritual love toward those who practice religions different from our own, expressed while still living on the earthly plane, will help immensely in this regard, giving us a leg up into Devachan -- for we will certainly be required to show in the heavenly realm that we have been tolerant, supportive and respectful of the views of others during physical life.

On the soul's trajectory from Devachan to rebirth, the starry heavens remain inside of us, an exquisite vision transmuted into our very souls. The moon and other planets, via the experiences we have had in other realms, become our organs for the next life, to the degree that we have spiritually expanded into willingness to take them in. The Sun, in this way, becomes the human heart, and its spiritual center thus journeys with us throughout earthly life. After death, we grow monumentally into ourselves; the spiritual, carried within during earthly life, grows to encompass our every surrounding. A soul is found to be lacking in Devachan if any sort of antipathy toward another is carried over to the next world. This shortcoming remains in the soul until the actions causing it can be either absolved or remedied, and it is felt as a sharp pang, a terrible disappointment in oneself, a failure that must be dealt with through the assumption of heavy responsibility. It is up to us, urgently, to remove mistakes and misdeeds from our karma while living in the physical world, as soon as the awareness strikes our consciousness that they exist.

It may seem that immoral or materialistic souls, looking back over their memories, are faced in the afterlife with a simplistic depiction of their misdeeds in the Akashic chronicle, spread out before them; but the experience, viewed in this way, falls far short of reality. Instead, the dead rely upon the living for their broader vision, so they can see something other than just themselves carrying out the experiences they lived during their previous earthly lives. This is why Anthroposophy so strongly recommends reading to the dead, one or several at a time, with or without a book, to help them become unstuck from incidences of myopic earthly perspective. While reading, be sure to ensconce your thoughts solidly in the realm of the spiritual. It is very difficult to actually learn more about spiritual science after death, because in order for this to occur, ideas are necessary, and the soul has already shed the intellect; but if a departed soul has heard and begun to understand a little of spiritual science already, the living can certainly help by reading cycles of anthroposophical lectures. The information will then be absorbed by the departed one at the level of feeling. Anthroposophy must be approached, even if only through an unconscious willingness of the soul, in the physical realm, in order for any advancement to be made in later realms.

Another option exists to provide enlightenment to such souls, but it is quite rare. Bodhisattvas can be described as uplifted, "lofty human beings" who are very advanced. They incarnate repeatedly on earth, and are "spiritual benefactors of mankind," able to teach both the living and the dead. After the physical death of Bodhisattvas, they can sometimes help other souls already in Devachan, to a limited extent. In this way, an unenlightened soul has a second chance at regaining its course and attaining the knowledge needed for progression to the next life.

In Devachan, we experience everything as outer phenomena, even our own inner selves. We actually have the capability of joining our beloved ones to an extent even more profound than that available to us on earth. Our dear ones also appear as vision; in fact, they *are* vision. Just as the color red, in the physical world, is perceived as coming from the rose, vision, in the heavenly realms, derives entirely from the spiritual. If we have withheld love from someone, we must find a way to give it while we are still on the physical plane. We cannot change or repair relationships beyond the commencement of the first period after Kamaloka. We can only observe, and resolve to manifest constructive, healing change in the next life. In the spiritual world, relationships take on a sense of permanency, because they continue just as they did on earth.

During earthly life, thoughts enter into our souls and become *feeling*. Many church sermons do not rise to the task of conveying this possibility, because of the way in which they are spoken, but the cultivation of exquisite religious feeling is the key to creating a connection with the Divine. After death, we can only enter into karma more deeply, so our lives must be lived out with the closest and truest possible connection to heaven that we can manifest from the physical plane.

CHAPTER VIII

The Essential Role of Christ and Alignment with Buddha

After death, we face the full effects of the moral principles we held during life, the consequences of our religious beliefs, and the awareness that our soul would be dimmed without the Mystery of Golgotha. "Christ gave mankind certainty that a spark of the divine continues to live in the human soul." We must not seek holiness, however, exclusively within ourselves. A true understanding and acceptance of Christ during physical life plants within us, like a promise or a seed, the powers and energies that can be used after death to retain consciousness between lives. With the mystery of Golgotha, we can remember occurrences across separate lives, and use spiritual perception while we are on earth to gain the faith-based impressions and feelings we will need to cross the abyss after death.

The Mystery of Golgotha occurred as an actual occult reality, and it has no effect on the non-denominational nature of Anthroposophy, which is defined as spiritual nourishment. Simply put, "Christ accompanies us, and thus we are capable of remembering." We must unite ourselves with Christ in order to remember earth and advance properly through the heavenly realms. Christ is considered by Anthroposophy to be the ruling Sun spirit. If we understand the mystery of Golgotha, we become acquainted with the positive Sun spirits as we traverse that sphere. They illumine us, and we become radiant with their light, permeated with it. We live, in this sphere, utterly filled with the light and the essence of Christ. We try to live correctly and well, allowing perceived differences between all souls to melt away. We endeavor not just to remember our true connection with Christ, but to carry Him within our souls at all times.

101

In primeval times, our ancient, original wisdom served us, as we passed through the Sun sphere, to help with our understanding of its purpose. A common core of the old knowledge still existed within us. Souls, upon entering the Sun sphere, formerly found themselves in their "primal home: the source of all human life." Even in physical life today, we still instinctively know this to be true. The sun feeds all life, and without it, we could not live. Humans who lived on Earth before the mystery of Golgotha were also able to recognize Christ in the Sun sphere, even though He had not yet come to earth, because of their possession of the ancient knowledge.

Then, in the "middle period of the earth," the ability to automatically understand the Sun sphere somehow eroded away and was lost, and could only be replaced through a spiritual event. The human soul community no longer rises to the Sun spontaneously after death, so we need the Mystery of Golgotha to allow us to prepare ourselves for life in the Sun sphere -- the ultimate, most magnificent spiritual community.

Ancient knowledge about the Sun sphere had fallen away, so a link to human consciousness and the Sun sphere had to be re-initiated and made possible once again. The true, complete meaning of the Christ mystery has only been discovered, through occultism and Anthroposophy, in modern times. With a solid, internalized understanding of the Mystery of Golgotha, we can again "move freely in the Sun sphere."

Today, people across the world perceive the essence and foundation of Christianity as a state of selflessness. Christ was accepted in the West not as a familiar divine being, but as an almost "alien personality" from far away. This type of faith demonstrates the non-egoic nature of Christianity because as a religion in the West, it did not arise out of its own locality or generational tradition. The universality of Christianity is demonstrated in the fact that

Christ "poured His being over the earth" for the benefit of *all* human souls, and therefore His significance is the same for everyone, regardless of religion.

Through Christianity, we are able to ask ourselves about every human being we meet: *how much of Christ is in that person?* At the same time, if we limit ourselves to enclosure within one religion only, it becomes wholly possible that we will remain alone within that particular limitation in the spiritual realm. Wide acceptance and understanding of other systems of faith becomes necessary for human, planetary and universal harmony and health.

When Christ left the Sun sphere and came to earth, His throne in the Sun was not, after that time, occupied by the wholeness and completeness of Christ. As humans, we must now bring from the earth what there is of Christ within us; in this way, we can experience a living relationship with Him in the Sun sphere to match the Akashic reality that is painted across the heavens. As Christians in Devachan, we begin to "live into" the people we knew on earth, and into the Higher Hierarchies, as well. We can then can experience the Christ within us and find at our disposal all of the necessary spiritual resources to travel through the Sun sphere in the correct manner. The Mystery of Golgotha is essential to our present evolutionary period because human souls need to evolve in the best possible way through the Sun sphere. With the goal, then, of later growing even further beyond the Sun, we must be capable of grasping all religions and thereby understanding every human soul.

We must understand equally the impulses of Christ and the impulses of those in opposition to Him: Lucifer and Arhiman. It is essential, in order to distinguish between them with our spiritual sight that we learn to "discern the essential *being* rather than the essential *teaching*." Christ showed us more through His actions than through His statements. It is not a question, then, of mere words that anyone could speak, but of *how* they are spoken and the feeling they impart. Jesus said, "Be conscious that you are like the Gods", and Lucifer said, "Ye shall be as Gods". It is crucial for the human soul, by feeling and knowing, to be able to distinguish easily between the two. "In the Sun sphere, the greatest danger is to take Lucifer for Christ, because both use the same language." "Everything depends upon the being speaking — not the doctrine."

It is only possible to distinguish between Christ and Lucifer, at this stage, through Anthroposophy. In order to tell the two apart in the spiritual world, it is not just the content of what is said that is important; the context is most crucial. This is the "deep cosmic mystery" inherent in the human conceptualization and acceptance of Christ. In order to distinguish between Christ and Lucifer, we must have acquired on earth a full and deep understanding of Christ, and we must have brought Him into our souls. We must also possess an intellectual and spiritual understanding of who Lucifer is, because he, in his more ancient and less harmful self, will be the one to lead us to the next spheres after the Sun.

"The firmament, after death, is filled with what we truly are in heart and mind," and this comes about according to whether we have fully accepted the mystery of Golgotha into our deepest selves. If we have done this, there has occurred "an all-around strengthening process", and we will be safe from all possible spiritual danger, including that posed by Lucifer.

After leaving the Sun sphere in Devachan, we must keep the Christ-impulse precious, close and clear in our memory so that Lucifer does not again become dangerous. For this, there exists a definite formula: the more we have received Christ in life, the stronger we will be in Devachan.

After the Sun sphere, the ego has further liberated itself because of its sequential progress through Devachan. Meanwhile, Christ, the Sun Spirit, descends to earth, and the human ego, approaching rebirth, joins the substance of Christ. Humans also experience a full immersion into the energy of Jesus after they have passed from the earthly realm.

Christ, in fact, is the total source of consciousness after death. Jesus united himself with earth; and, after death, if we are united with Him in Devachan, we will experience all of the spiritual beauty He brought about and witnessed on earth.

Our bodily nature, unfortunately, has been in decline since the time of Christ. People used to be more clairvoyant; our bodies were stronger, tougher and more resilient. At the end of human evolution, at this rate, "our bodily nature will be most barren." Similarly, human soul decline began at humanity's bodily peak -- the Greek epoch. The Greeks were perfectly happy with their idealized physical life, and did not work on the spiritual level as deeply.

Over the course of the development of the earth, the spiritual height, of humanity came about through the mystery of Golgotha. As this gift united itself with earth evolution, human beings began a spiritual ascension that, today, has really only just begun. Eventually, humanity will rise to the original spiritual height it had attained before being led astray by Lucifer.

When a total renewal of the life of the human soul became necessary, Christ came to us through the mystery of Golgotha, a blast of spiritual light radiating through all human souls. Without this act, human beings would have continued to experience dramatic loss of soul fragments along with any trace of our total spiritual heritage.

Infinite possibilities still exist for the further development of

Christianity here on Earth. Anthroposophy is not just a teaching; it is a *responsibility* that keeps us in touch with one another across the worlds. On earth, humankind is still divided into races and nations; but in the future, this will continue to change, and we will merge together into a state of divine understanding. Already, "in the west, egoistic religion has disappeared" through Christianity and human beings continue to evolve through Anthroposophy. It is of great importance that Christianity be conceptualized not through conversion, but by looking for that which is Christian in all human beings. In Devachan, "in the true knowledge of Christ, all men can come together in the Sun sphere" and we must, to the greatest extent possible, mirror this heavenly event on the earthly plane.

In the Sun sphere, we become our God selves. We find two thrones: that of Lucifer, who tries to tempt us, and the empty throne of Christ. His energy there now manifests as an "Akashic picture of Christ", and it is a blessing for us to find. Interestingly, we are only able to find this picture of Christ in the Sun sphere now, because of His previous descent to earth to live in human form. In the Akashic picture, we see and learn a great deal from the deeds He performed while He was still on the Sun.

In order to progress this far in our awareness, the mystery of Golgotha must enter into both our astral and etheric bodies. We draw from the Sun sphere what we need in order to choose our proper astral body for the next life. Christ, while still in the Sun, was well-known to ancient, pre-Christian spiritual and religious leaders. In the future, people will deprive themselves of proper experiences of the Sun sphere if they do not have an understanding of Christ. It depends upon how we *let* it act upon us, how we allow it to form our astral and etheric bodies in the right way.

In the Devachanic plane, we must internalize all of this knowledge and carry it over to Mars from the Sun sphere. When we experience true recognition of self in this way, we access a deep sense of security, belonging and relief. We gain the awareness that we belong to the whole macrocosm, that we are part of it and that it resides also within us. The Christ impulse exists as the guiding impulse of this awareness.

In Anthroposophy, Christ may be viewed as the second, spiritual Adam. Through Him, soul content is "poured into the I". There are still a number of people in the world who possess "some of the ancient spiritual treasure", but they are few. Before Golgotha, humankind was more dependent upon the angels, who have now learned to "guide and lead...in a free way" according to the growing independence and free will of the human being. Angels who have kept pace with the evolution of humankind can approach us, but those who have not appear in our psychic vision as hazy, remote or indefinable.

Public opinion, considered by Anthroposophy to be one of the most severely limiting and draining earthly influences upon the essential life force, actually developed only four to five centuries ago in the shape it takes today. It exerts "extraordinary power over the individual" and has the power, if we let it, to undermine our entire existence, reducing our life accomplishments to a mere shadow of what they could have been. In previous centuries, humans were not as apt to put faith in intangible authority. The current godlike authority of doctors can be taken as an example of this type of thinking. Public opinion, formed by the troublemaking "backward (spirits) of the lowest sphere", must be balanced in the afterlife with some kind of compensatory measure.

Luciferic spirits have no real power over us after Kamaloka because they stand hidden, unwilling to pass by the mystery of Golgotha. Further evolution of humankind will originate from improvement of the inner self and a development of the type of strength that can only manifest through Anthroposophy. The Christ impulse leads us through this process in the Mars sphere, and helps us to drop the need for favorable public opinion, which only causes people to become compliant and uniform, rather than free and independent.

In earthly life, it is exceedingly important to avoid one-sided, intellectually-based positions. For balance, both poles must be present in all human consideration. Humankind is in the process of manifesting new spiritual capacities, and those who do this successfully will become the most advanced souls.

Buddha, in alliance with Christ, plays a spiritual role in the initiation of such peaceful thinking, and results of the time spent with him in Devachan may only become apparent later in physical life. Earthly souls influenced by Buddha will act as catalysts of future spiritual progress, and they will be late bloomers, spiritually speaking. A midlife series of epiphanies may cause their spiritual strength to come to the fore in a way that cannot be ignored. They are the new helpers of humanity. This kind of positive and peaceful change does not appear to result from a person's own physical incarnation, but to be delivered independently as a gift from Spirit.

Of all the gods, only Christ knows death. This is most significant. As we have seen, the time immediately following physical death can feel very similar to a great earthly loneliness, if one is without connections to prepare for the spiritual world. In fact, death is totally absent in the heavenly realm, and nothing can be learned of it there. Angels avert their gaze so as not to see the mysteries of death, which only Christ experienced. He alone of all "superhuman, supra-sensory beings" went through this portal, and only He fully understands what it is like to die. Most angelic beings live purely in the heavenly realms, never coming to Earth even as human souls, and therefore never going through physical death. Christ Himself was never on

Earth before His advent; He had no previous lives here.

In the Sun sphere, as on Earth, we must find Christ and recognize Him in order to process our soul work and proceed according to the greater good. Christianity is unlimited, and available to all, so anyone on the earthly plane can choose this path. Whenever we meet other human beings on Earth, we can make the effort to see Jesus is living in them, just as He lives within every human being.

Christ did not go through initiation here on earth -- He was initiated simply *by virtue of being here*. We must understand this fact within the context of the earthly realm and within the boundaries of our physical lives in order to better see and experience Him in the spiritual world. This differs from experiences with Buddha, whom souls may encounter in the heavenly realms just as they might have done at some point within the earthly realm.

We all travel through cosmic universes after death. If one has received the golden light of Christ during earthly life, one can receive the silvery light of Buddha after death, even if the soul never had the chance to meet him here on earth. "Fresh impulses will continually enter human evolution", and Buddha is one of these.

St. Francis of Assisi was, in a previous incarnation, Buddha; and it can be noticed that followers of the Buddha and St. Francis hold many similarities. Additionally, the Angels' Song of Peace at the birth of Jesus was Buddha's contribution to the mystery of Golgotha. It was sung as an inscription into Christ's mission, and represented Buddha's work at the birth of Christ. Buddha continues to work upon earthly souls, even now. Buddha received the Christ impulse, and was no longer concerned with Buddhism in its original form; he became an "assistant to Christian evolution."

In the course of his spiritual trajectory, Buddha became for Mars what Christ has become for the Earth. Mars, in essence, gained its own savior. Until the 15th and 16th centuries, Mars had been descending solely into the material. This phenomenon brought the knowledge of science to earth, but if the trend had continued unchecked, humanity would have also become divided into two groups: the material versus the spiritual. Additionally, the spiritual group would have been entirely unable to take part in the material plane on earth.

Christian Rosenkreutz, in his time, wanted to make it possible for every human being to ascend to spiritual heights, and he sent Buddha back to humankind as St. Francis of Assisi, so that we could again benefit from his spiritual light. He also sent Buddha to Mars, where he now works on behalf of all humans. This can be viewed as a "Mystery of Golgotha on Mars", though it is not as powerful or pervasive as Christ's influence on the earthly sphere.

"The Buddha element" can now be taken up by human souls passing through Mars. One can consider that Buddha was, in essence, crucified on the most warlike of all planets. He preceded Jesus in earthly time, and continued to work on humanity thereafter, all the way up to the present. Buddha's kingdom on Mars helps with the temperance of public opinion, which only really matters to human beings living on earth. He helps us to release it and to free ourselves so that our true life purpose can come forward, unhesitant and unafraid. The lessons Buddha taught on earth unfold, in their progressed form, on Mars as well, and assist very meaningfully in preparing the soul for eventual reincarnation.

CHAPTER IX

The Higher Hierarchies and Archangel Michael

After death, we meet directly with the Higher Hierarchies, angels, archangels and certain elemental beings. It is common, in our time, for people to neglect deeper thought and consideration of life after death, and a simplistic view of heaven only ingrains this particular line of thinking; but it is certain that if we go through earthly life without an ethical view of the afterlife, we will, in fact, be entirely unable to meet angelic beings after we have passed.

Beings of the Higher Hierarchies give to us essential energies with which to re-enter physical existence. Human souls must bring these gifts with them between worlds. We are "attracted by mixture with the hereditary stream", as well as by the impulse toward our own reincarnation in a physical body, but this is all secondary to pure soul evolution. When we do reincarnate, forces brought from the spiritual world, in the form of beautiful visions, refine our souls for further evolution. Human beings, on our own, are wholly responsible for our own earthly choices, and we have to be willing to work hard at the construction of our own destiny. This includes not just the destiny common to our physical reality, but that of our spiritual selves, as well.

Above humanity on the earthly plane, there exists a realm of heavenly beings. These magnificent spirits, usually thought of and referred to as angels, are "a continuation of the four stages found on earth" (plant, animal, vegetable, mineral), and represent "a primeval world wisdom" comprised of everything humans can possibly perceive, including that which can only be perceived by means of clairvoyance.

111

In fact, everything we experience on earth is "prefigured in deed and in knowledge by the beings who stand above us." Everything that exists in the world was originally contained in the thoughts of God and His messengers, the Higher Hierarchies; and the creation of our world came about through their work, assistance and wisdom.

In the first post-Atlantean culture, the Vedas of ancient India received knowledge of the higher beings. Today, deeper powers of comprehension are needed to understand original cosmic wisdom. Angels also appeared in ancient Persia, Chaldea and Egypt, and finally in the Christianity of our time. The "stream of ancient wisdom...never dried up." It came to us to increasingly through the earthly appearance of Christ, who brought this knowledge and understanding in renewed, revivified form. It is also contained within living cultural wisdom, in the context of mystery societies like the brothers of the Holy Grail, which once had access to information that was previously unavailable to the greater part of humanity.

This same primeval cosmic wisdom can now be brought through to a greater number of people because of important spiritual events that allow it to be understood, considered and spoken about more freely. Rosicrucian knowledge, for example, contains all Eastern wisdom, renewed (though not repeated) through the Christ impulse. Buddha's description of the suffering of life was all true, but Christ gave us a means by which the suffering could cease; as a result, there remains no real reason, in our time, for theoretical opposition between religions.

Ancient wisdom must now be accepted once again, though now it is more difficult to understand because so much time has elapsed. The Atlanteans possessed the old clairvoyance, if a bit dimmed from its original brilliance. Humans, in the Atlantean time, did not see just the physical stars when gazing into the heavens; they saw the actual aura of each planet — something of its true essence. They saw spiritual beings and hierarchies everywhere, including the spiritual beings specifically associated with each celestial body, and spoke between themselves only of spiritual content. When speaking of a planet, they referred not to the physical planet, but to a spiritual world with spiritual beings -- the most important consideration when conceptualizing the occult planets. In the Dionysian mysteries, Venus represented the Arcchi; Mars, the Mights; the Sun, the Powers; Jupiter, the Dominions; and Saturn, the Thrones.

The old names denoting spiritual meaning were then forgotten, and began to refer mostly to physical matter. The spiritual and materialistic planes have continued to become distant and even polarized from one another. We must now begin again to see the universe with an awareness originating from our innermost self instead of from the outer, more physically-oriented gaze. Information about the Angels, Archangels and Thrones, largely forgotten and without a point of reference, can still be accessed, but we must use the third eye, our clairvoyant consciousness. The connections between the worlds must be renewed.

In the Bhagavad Gita, it is written that souls going through the gate of death during the height of the day need not return to earth, but those who die at night must return. This passage of the sacred book has been rejuvenated through Christianity in the following manner.

In ancient times, all was referred back to the four elements. The natural phenomena most important in ancient world was fire, or the fourth element. According to Anthroposophy, "fire is so rarified that it permeates all other elements." It is the inner and outer manifestation of warmth, "the first stage at which matter becomes soul", a bridge between the worlds, a portal. Light and smoke occur when an object is lit on fire; and light is not actually seen by the physical eye without another object or reference point from which to base our perception. In spiritual science, "we rise upward from earth to water; from air to fire; and then to light." We proceed from the visible to the invisible. "Fire is on the boundary between what is outwardly perceptible and material, and what is etheric-spiritual", or invisible. The payment for the crossing is smoke. In burning, the rules of nature dictate that "warmth produces light, but also produces opaque, dark matter". Hence the spiritual warmth of fire, enchanted into smoke along with the elemental beings.

Elemental beings are sent to earth by higher divine, formative beings. At the beginning of the earth, all elementals had to descend from fire and become embedded in other matter. Hence, everything on earth can be conceived of as "densified fire".

If we live life in a state of unawareness, the elemental beings enter and permanently inhabit us, trapped; but if we are fully aware and actively thinking, we redeem the elemental being, and raise it to its former incarnation. "We release enchanted beings, or imprison them in our inner being, with no transformation having taken place within them." When a human goes through of gate of death, untransformed elementals have gained nothing, but transformed ones can return to their original sphere. Human beings are fully capable of freeing such elemental beings: this is accomplished in a release similar to the kindling of flames from mere smoking tinder, with our attention fixed upon the fire we have released them to. This represents a true understanding of ancient rituals.

This is the Bhagavad Gita passage explained, describing the destiny of elemental spirits. "Materialism binds elementals to us, forcing them to be connected to us over & over again." The elementals bring about day and night. The creativity and energy in people become increasingly beneficial, attracting beings of light, which are then led back into the day. We can release darker elementals back to the night. If we carry darker elementals over as a result of apathy, they will be reincarnated with us — and vice-versa. We are equally capable of bringing beings of light through and releasing them. If we are contented and serene in life, we free harmonious elemental beings. The mood of the soul releases or imprisons spirits accordingly.

Elementals of the Sun are responsible for summer, while winter beings remain chained, or enchanted, throughout their season and the year. With the approach of Christmas, if people carry goodness and warmth alive in their hearts, they can help to release the winter elementals to freedom.

The vastness of primeval wisdom is revealed in this call to action. "We influence the whole cosmos in all we do, even down to our moods." We have, therefore, a "heightened sense of responsibility", and must take the importance and preciousness of life very seriously in order to ascend to the height of our own spiritual possibility.

Saturn, the Sun, the Moon and Earth represent four planetary incarnations of their own, because each planet once reincarnated into the next. The former planetary incarnation of the Moon does not designate our moon, but refers to a stage in its past existence. On Earth, we have become human and thereby "I" beings. On other planets, the Gods, the Angels and all of the Hierarchies were once human beings. As human beings ourselves, we must be willing to do the work to grow and to spiritually transform; for in our present, earthly state, we are not yet gods. There exists a clearly defined hierarchy of spiritual beings, as outlined below:

Angels are nonphysical beings who exist one degree above humanity. They were once human, when they lived on the Moon.

Archangels exist two degrees above humanity in the hierarchy. They are beings of fire, and were once human on the Sun. They act as spiritual messengers to humankind.

The Archai, or *Spirits of Personality* exist three degrees above humanity. They were once human on Saturn.

The Higher Hierarchies have a rich and extremely ancient history, from the dawn of time. They "built their whole bodies from warmth and fire", and their "inner warmth of soul" was originally felt on Saturn, in its early evolution. There, "inner warmth transformed itself gradually into perception of outer warmth" as the evolution of the Higher Hierarchies commenced and Saturn began its transformation.

The Archai had the ability to transform outer warmth into inner warmth. They came into being as "warmth eggs" on Saturn, which looked, at the time, much like a raspberry or a blackberry. The planet was breathing in and out, aspirating fire instead of air. Many of the Archai preferred to leave some of the warmth behind in order to become human, and also so they could differentiate themselves from their environment and "create a realm next to their own". This assisted in the development of "I" consciousness, and allowed Saturn to continue to exist after its great transformation.

Higher beings intervened to dissolve Saturn so that it could move into its next incarnation. A lower realm was left behind, and a long phase of night was followed by dawn. The Sun state of Saturn then arose. The Archai were bound to the planet they had left behind, and they were drawn down into a new planetary existence. They created

116

their own karma on a re-born Saturn: the Sun. Winds, air and gases blew with random force in every direction.

"Light appeared for the first time during the course of the planets' transformations". The deeds of the archangels gained them the possibility of becoming visible. They incorporated their bodies of gas, air and inner light *from* light. They were, quite literally, made of air, fire and light. Now they could differentiate their bodies from the Sun, but "preferred to remain in the Sun substance", because they liked their bodies as they had made them.

When they inhaled, all was dark, and night fell; as they exhaled, light would appear along with the day. The sun went through "a real breathing process", and was not constantly light and fiery as it is today.

The Archai – the "beginnings", or primal angels – created planets in new forms. The Archangels became "the heralds of the cosmos" and achieved their humanity on the Sun, which had been left for them by the Archai. The forces that were working in the Archai on ancient Saturn were the same as those now causing human power of conceptual thought, though their abilities in this area were far greater than ours are today. They were much like wizards, and incredibly powerful.

The Saturn fire pulled inward as internal soul fire, then ascended to higher realms, to be reborn on the Sun. The Archai got this form, warmth and fire of the Sun from even higher beings: *the Thrones.* This allowed the archangels to "achieve their human stage on the old Sun," where they "absorbed and streamed out light".

Human beings incarnate, as we have seen, with physical, etheric, astral and "I" bodies. When entering the spiritual world, the astral

117

body becomes the 'I', and the physical body becomes the etheric (life body, or Buddhi). Later, the human being becomes a spiritual being: seven-fold, and ruled by the "I". The process ascends higher and higher as the human being relinquishes the act of taking and reverts purely to giving, thereby becoming a greater being, capable of giving in the cosmic sense.

Between the Thrones and the Archai exist still other beings: *the Powers. The Mights* (the Dunamis) are one stage higher. Still higher are *the Dominions,* and then *the Thrones.* Each level acts as angels to the level below them. *With each planetary transformation or reincarnation, each level of being evolved one level higher.*

Archangels enjoy floating out into the cosmos, rather than contracting or densifying. They prefer to dwell in the light ether. They prolonged their stay in the universe with the assistance of beings higher than the Thrones: *the Cherubim,* described as "especially sublime spiritual beings" who help the Archangels.

The Cherubim were conceived of by the Post-Atlanteans in four definite etheric forms: winged lion, bull, eagle, and human. They approached the old Sun, which was still following its rhythm of night and day, from four different directions and established the first seeds of the animal kingdom. On Saturn, the first seeds of the human body had already been born. The animal forms became "the sun's reflection of the zodiac".

Naming, in ancient times, expressed the true nature of the being, and the names of animals were given with deep thought and consideration. Each Cherubim has four companions. The eagle took the name Scorpio due to a subsequent transformation within the zodiac. The human took the name Water Man (Aquarius).

In order for the archangels to continue their course by day, the Cherubim had to continue theirs at night, producing animal beings standing below the level of humanity as a form of compensation. A lowering process had to take place whenever there was an ascension.

Ancient Saturn had "nothing to do with our present Saturn", because everything was present embryonically on ancient Saturn, a vast, "gigantic body of warmth". The Cherubim were already present there at the periphery, but had not yet accomplished "the high task" of transmutation.

Saturn was a "globe of warmth surrounded by *Choirs* of exalted beings"; it transformed itself into Old Sun, then Old Moon. Our earth came about when it separated out of the sun. Even beings now cut off from the sun still develop their "sun singularities". We will eventually unite with the sun again. Saturn is different from all other planets: darkness, seen through light, appears in blue as the planetary rings. It embodies neutral, soul warmth as well as physical warmth; it is, therefore, composed solely of warmth.

The seven sequential stages of human development are as follows: Saturn, Sun, Moon, Earth, Jupiter, Venus, and Vulcan (the highest spiritual degree). The Sun will eventually sacrifice itself, and become a choir of beings, for each choir of beings must first have existed as a solar system.

The Seraphim exist above the Cherubim. They are the beings who receive many of the highest directives from the Gods.

The order of Hierarchies, below God, looks like this:

The Choirs

The Seraphim

The Cherubim

The Thrones

The Dominions

The Mights

The Powers, or Spirits of Form, have a special mission: they guide us from one planetary condition to another. After humanity has become so spiritual that it will no longer belong to the earth, the Powers will help us to advance to Jupiter.

The Archai, or primal powers, are the "time spirits" of any particular age. They help planets to incarnate into new forms, govern the interrelationships of the entire human species on earth, and can "transform themselves and take on a different spiritual body". They are responsible for governing the "significance and mission of a given human epoch". They keep people to their assigned era. According to the laws of the universe, the right souls must appear at the right time, and the Archai regulate this.

The Archangels bring human souls into harmonious order. As "folk spirits" for humankind, the archangels are capable of manifesting on the earthly plane, simultaneously guarding whole populations. "Cosmic conditions" affecting the physical characteristics of humans are also governed by the archangels.

The Angels

Human spiritual evolution began during the ancient Lemurian era.

Most people do not remember previous lives, unless they are clairvoyant; but the angels can remember everything. They are our guardian beings, and though they do not order karma, they guide us through its process in safety and security. Even if we do not remember the primeval knowledge from the beginning of our evolution, we can ask our angel for details, wisdom and guidance, as it is dictated by God. They respect our free will, and will not intervene in karmic matters of the soul unless asked. Angels are responsible for guiding us from incarnation to incarnation.

Spheres of Influence

The Thrones: Saturn

The Dominions: Jupiter

The Mights: Mars

The Powers: Sun

The Archai: Venus

The Archangels: Mercury

The Angels: Earth to Moon

The Anthroposophical system with regard to the planets is different than the astronomical one because in it, the earth is taken as the starting point, and stands at the center of all of the other planets. Human beings were obligated to establish astronomy, on the physical plane, in order to understand space and the universe. The spiritual system will once again be accepted one day, because everything in the universe is spiritually dependent upon the earth. In spiritual sight, the earth, not the sun, is central.

There exists a "flowing-down of the fire substance" along the line of the Higher Hierarchies. When an old solar system dies, sometime in the future, the Seraphim will have reached their highest point; they will then have to choose another sphere in which to work.

The Second Hierarchy is not as evolved as the upper realm of the Higher Hierarchies. The Dominions, or Spirits of Wisdom, are the organizers. The Mights (Virtues, or Spirits of Movement) carry out directives. The Powers, or Spirits of Form, ensure that form is preserved and maintained, and prevent it from disappearing. They receive what needs to be transformed, and carry out the regulation of information as given by God.

The Second Hierarchy was "inside the Saturn substance" at the beginning of its evolution, when spiritual energies were responsible for its rotation. The higher beings worked from the periphery, while those not as elevated in the hierarchy worked from within. The Thrones were the first to affect ancient Saturn. They poured "warmth substance" into it, creating "warmth eggs". The Powers, the Mights and the Dominions were active from within; the Cherubin, Seraphim and Thrones worked from the outside. The eggs began to rotate until they came back to their starting point, then stopped, and falling onto each other, created a unified globe over the course of time.

During the transformation from ancient Saturn to Old Sun, primeval form became gas or air, a "fire mist or fire air". The Dominions then compressed Saturn, which was as large as our present solar system, until it became smaller.

Old Moon arose through further condensation from Old Sun. It introduced and regulated the watery element. The Mights brought this about during their reign; they compressed Old Sun to create it anew. Wherever beings develop in the universe, there are those who advance and those who choose to remain where they are. During, the compression of Old Sun, the Mights were at a different stage of maturity, and the two classes separated. The more advanced energy drew out the Sun, and those who stayed back formed Old Moon by contracting it.

The dwelling places of the higher beings are not actually *on* the planets mentioned, but within their spheres. "The planets mark the boundaries of these realms." Our experience in earthly life, with regard to the angels, is similar to that of a small child in relation to a mature adult. Beings living within the spheres descended to the earth to impart lessons to humankind in Atlantean and Lemurian times, when higher beings were "teachers of a youthful humankind." In this way, the angels "piloted" the human species.

The manos, or spirit self, represents the transformed astral body. It is not something newly added, but the "transformed product" of the process. The transformed etheric body is called the Buddhi, and the transformed physical body is called the Ahtman. This diagram cannot be applied to the angels. They have a physical, etheric and astral *totality*, plus a separate "I", or manos, which is not developed. An angel's physical aspect is visible in the supersensible world in the form of mist, wind, water and lightning. The bodies of the angels do not need to have a definite spiritual boundary. They can float, hover, appear hazy or indistinct, and are made up of far more than just a materially perceived image. The angels dwell within everything, in infinite ways. Dozens of angels, for example, could have their densest physical nature in one body of water. As humans, we need clairvoyant sight in the astral world in order to see their soul spiritual nature.

Among the Archangels, the astral body is not required to be connected to a visible or etheric body. "They have a spiritual part above, and a reflection of the spiritual below." The physical body and etheric body can only be united if the physical body consists of air (or wind) and fire.

The Archai possess a physical body below, and all the rest above. They can only be perceived in fire. In a flash of lightning, we see all that we can see of their bodies; this is because the lightning actually contains their physical bodies.

In the case of the Powers, the Sun makes use of beings made of both fire and wind.

In Lemurian times, humans did not have physical bodies any more than the angels did. We had only etheric and astral bodies, and could not quite manage ourselves on earth yet. Inhabitants of Venus (the *Spirits of Personality*) radiated into and inspired certain human beings during this time period. Because they possessed a different physical body from other human beings, these individuals made a strong impression upon everyone around them. They became "objects of awe, reverence, obedience". Speech and signs were quite unnecessary then, due to the innate strength of human psychic powers.

Archangels, in Atlantean times, could "ensoul and enliven" human beings. Certain people who lived then looked just the same as everyone else, but were "ensouled" by archangels, and gave heavenly laws to the world. Ancient Atlantean mystery centers rose up, where oracles were witnessed and pronounced. These centers could then draw even more human beings to them in order to train them. Some humans were actually archangels, and were also visible, in a type of reflection or second form, as gigantic beings behind

124

their human physical forms. After death, in these cases, the etheric body did not dissolve; the archangels simply returned to higher worlds.

In the Post-Atlantean period, selected leaders were sometimes ensouled by angels, giving them the power to look, during their human lives, back over their past incarnations. The Maya incarnated as humans who were actually altogether different from how they appeared to be on earth, because "angels spoke through them," and they possessed intensely magnified powers of extrasensory perception.

There also lived human beings through whom the angels and archangels could speak spontaneously. Higher beings could emancipate human beings through teachings of primeval wisdom. Through clairvoyant consciousness, we can, to this day, see visions of angels and orbs "observed in their living soul-spiritual state".

Old Saturn was as large as our present-day solar system, and when it became the sun, the zodiac surrounded it. Represented by the Cherubim, Seraphim and Thrones, the constellations indicated the direction in which certain beings could be found, acting as "signposts" for human beings gazing into the night sky:

The Lion emerged as the heart, as life itself, and permanently inhabited the zone in space where it had first originated. This constellation may be identified both inwardly and outwardly.

The Crab represents the breastplate surrounding the heart.

The Scorpion: Because Old Sun was the sacrifice of the Dominions, it contracted and became more dense. The region of the Scorpion inflicted the death sting upon Old Sun; this is the area in space where destructive impulses come from. Under the sign of Scorpio, the slaying of each of the planets took place.

The Water Man lives in the sphere of Mars, a "compressed globe of water". Human beings receive consciousness here in their travel between death and rebirth.

The Bull: Earth is separated from the sun with "lunar dross". For ancient Lemurians, the initiation of the "I" in this zone represented the third period of Earth's development. This is history is reflected within Egyptian culture.

The current esoteric configuration of the planets represents their fourth state of development. Some aspects of each planet were left behind during the reshaping of the solar system, the occult form of which eventually took on the shape of a lentil. Spiritual beings or hierarchies were fully responsible for the formation and contraction of the planets.

We have seen that on ancient Saturn, the Spirits of Personality lived out their human stage of existence, though not in physical form; this stage came later. On Old Sun, the Archangels lived as humans; and on Old Moon, the Angels experienced their own human existence. The origin of each human body part and internal system is also represented in its own specific area in the stars. From this story of the birth of the solar system, we learn that the central answer to any question can only be understood after the periphery has also been understood. Karma is an inescapable factor, and things have to be dismantled, step by step, in reverse order, just as they were constructed. "The cosmic process of becoming is the creation of karma," and the process of dissolution is revealed in the suffering of karma. Groups of people, even whole nations, can accumulate collective karma during their growth.

The Angels and Archangels are the beings responsible for guiding humankind to a higher stage of evolution. After we have successfully built up to the zenith of our soul growth, other spiritual beings will take over. When this happens, leading personalities on earth "must take the accumulated karma of that nation on themselves". We will know when a higher stage in the development of true leaders has been reached, because we will see that their capacity to receive has transformed itself to a capacity to give. After death, in Kamaloka, anything we have not mastered during life automatically dissolves into the astral world, but not without consequence. Soul advancement can be considered as the ability to leave less and less behind in the spiritual world.

Human beings are gradually approaching the state of angels, but we will still require a great deal of time before this type of ascension can take place. After much soul advancement and working through of karma, the soul finally reaches the stage where it cannot harm anyone left on earth, and cannot leave behind anything in Kamaloka. In this case, "the whole of the astral body has become spiritualized." "The spirit self stamps itself into the etheric body" to leave an imprint of the astral body, so that no remnants of the etheric body are left behind.

When we demonstrate "mastery over astral and etheric bodies", the "I" can "dispose of these bodies freely" and sacrifice them, "transferring them to others". When freed souls want to return to earth, they can construct a new astral and etheric bodies with which to do so. Those who take on the astral and etheric bodies of others, on the other hand, can carry forward human missions according to Dharma law.

Humans will eventually reach higher stages of development, like the angels, but it will not be exactly the same; and in any case, before we are to arrive at that point, there must be further spiritual contribution to the world and far higher ascension of the soul.

Planetary structures also disappear once they have achieved what they need to achieve. Humanity will eventually be compelled to leave the earth, because there will be nothing further that the earth can offer to human development. What will remain after we leave? Will our imprint be of any significance to our old home planet?

The answer can be found in an examination of physical matter. Planets gradually contract; "matter impresses increasingly into the center and, remarkably, disappears into the center point," but it reappears at the outer circumference, or periphery. In this way, "nothing, absolutely nothing, is lost of what has been accomplished on a planet." When a beautiful landmark, for example, disappears, it will reappear on the other side of perception; and "in the intervening period, it is in another dimension." When this has happened to planetary structures in the past, their resident beings withdrew and went to live in another place in the universe. If one considers the cyclical lineage beginning with the Choirs and descending all the way down to the Angels, we can see that the Higher Hierarchies are actually our ancestors.

Beyond the Seraphim, Cherubim and Thrones exists the Holy Trinity, directly experiencing the "immediate gaze of the Godhead". These highest beings of the spiritual hierarchies were always within God's presence, and always will be. "They accomplish everything by gazing upon God, and God works through them." There is no need for deliberation or judgment. The Dominions, Mights and Powers (spirits of wisdom, movement and form) do not see directly into God's form, but receive direct impulses from Him, with slightly less strength.

During the war in Heaven, "adversely-commanded Mights" were put in the way of development, acting as obstacles so that certain events could come about that could not otherwise have manifested. Obstacles make one stronger. The forces originally at play were not evil forces, but sacrificed forces; They were gods of hindrance and impediment. These "countermanded dunamis" were not evil at first, but they eventually became the origin of evil as the tempters of Angels (when angels lived as humans on the Moon). The Angels chose to abstain from fighting and withdrew from the Moon, where the hindrances were present, and began to follow the Sun instead. Others, who remained, hardened themselves, and carried within their bodies the action of the adversely-commanded mights. Still others who remained behind were actually attracted to negativity in the form of Luciferic beings. This only happened because the Mights were given adverse orders by the Godhead, which wanted to strengthen the forces of good by means of a semi-sacrificial distraction through negative powers.

All of the angels began to work on humankind during the Lemurian time, and humans were then given the option to either ascend immediately or to move toward Luciferic beings. They were given the possibility of error or evil, and also the capacity for free will, allowing them to rise above both. If we consider the ascended angels who preferred to fly up to spiritual worlds, we may choose to meditate upon Archangel Michael. In fact, during the course of human existence, we are all called to be like him, to become a Michael.

A war in heaven occurred, and within it could be found the primeval, secret of the origin of evil. Archangel Michael fought the dragon, which was overthrown and tossed onto the earth. The battlefield was located between present Jupiter and Mars. During the 19th century, the devastation was discovered again, by science, in

129

the form of small planetoids. "The war in Heaven took place during the transition from the Sun to the Moon." Some angels refused to participate in evil; and in them, we find the possibility of freedom. Lucifer's influences try to enshroud the human "I", but the light shield of the angels encircles us and protects us from such influences.

Christ has advanced so far that He can penetrate the human being as far as the "I" (not just the etheric and astral body). The "I" expresses itself through the blood, which can be viewed as a remnant of the warmth of Old Saturn. We recall that Christ is a Sun being, streaming golden light and radiant warmth to the soul. With the passage of time, the human "I" will become more and more capable of overcoming the forces that want to pull it down. Christ had "no compulsion to bring people to Him". His greatest contribution was not what He taught, but what He *did*. His actions and His deeds made possible the efficacy of His teaching.

Any teaching can only have an impactful action upon the "I" when we "freely resolve to receive the Christ". In choosing Christ, we receive a divine power, not just a teaching. Our advancement must represent "a voluntary ascent into the higher world". This has been possible for humans only since the time when Christ was called upon to be a human being on earth.

Luciferic beings, on the other hand, should have been human beings on the Moon, but chose differently. Christ's light irradiates the human body and helps us to release Luciferic powers, which, through us, will one day also experience the power of Christ and be redeemed.

According to Anthroposophy, Christ is the "free helper" of human beings, not a god. Gradually, humanity will mature and become one of the Hierarchies. We will then be the first who are not automatically compelled to do what we are told; we possess free will and therefore the spiritual freedom to do good, of our own volition. Humanity can achieve its own cosmic ideal. In fact, "wisdom must become an ideal for us," allowing us to reach our own individual destiny in the proper manner.

The Angels live directly above our realm, and they are at the evolutionary stage of Jupiter. The Archangels live in the realm of Venus, and the Archai live in the Vulcan realm. Still higher, we find the Spirits of Form. They have already passed beyond the stages of the future that we can conceive of, and live at the eighth stage. Humans are currently at the fourth stage. These stages do not exist side by side, but actually share space, and permeate each other.

As humans, we go through life as if through water, only just keeping our heads above the surface. When we feel Luciferic forces, we are "yielding one-sidedly to fantasy and over-enthusiasm". Luciferic forces can manifest at the level of our blood; consider the figure of speech used when someone is angry and their *blood is boiling*. Simultaneously, humans can also experience a heavy, pressing-down sort of energy, a hardening force, a force that encourages us to blindly accept less than we know we deserve; these are the Arhimanic beings, and they can be present at the level of our bones.

Luciferic forces want "to make the world desert the divine beings", to cause humans to forsake what they feel is divine in themselves. This can be felt as an upward pull. Arhimanic powers want to gain control over human beings and make us dependent upon them; they include mankind in everything having to do with their sphere of power. This can be felt as a downward pull. These two forces of negativity also battle each other, using up some of their strength in a kind of civil war. We are caught in the middle, though we may be unaware of this fact, and "we must feel our divine essence" in order to survive spiritually. We exist at the center of the fulcrum. The scale of equilibrium is determined wholly by the Christ impulse and the degree to which we have internalized it during physical life. Negative powers want to conceal the secret of this triad, because human beings are fully capable of balancing it, thereby causing disruption in the aims of darker forces and transforming their intentions into light.

There exists great confusion about this triad; even Goethe confused the two negative powers. Throughout much of history, the dualistic concept of God versus the devil has stood in the place of proper understanding of the triad, which may be seen as the Christ impulse -- lived through humankind -- standing between two warring, negative forces. The dualistic view is illusory, because in the end, it actually allows "the removal of the divine from consciousness"; and allows the Luciferic principle to usurp the divine name of Heaven. Steiner called this "the great delusion of modern mankind". In this false world view, the simplistic dichotomy of heaven versus hell is actually the result of the Luciferic posing as the heavenly, all the while fighting Arhimanic forces that are posing as hell.

As a result of the strong existing divergence between these two concepts, Catholics have been banned from participating in Anthroposophy. Attempts at conversion, however, are to be avoided; at all costs, the triad must make its way through to world conceptualization under its own steam. We must also avoid the spiritual mistake of denouncing the actions of others as heresy. The Christ impulse can only be comprehended if it is perceived as the equilibrium in the triad; anything coming from the delusion of duality is not a true comprehension of Christ at all. This is related to the mission of Archangel Michael.

Tangible dangers to human soul life can come about as a result of this commonly-accepted duality of good versus evil, because people have erroneously intermixed the Luciferic and the Divine element. Academic life, especially, is devoid of soul: "mere theories will not build a bridge between the bodily and the spiritual." Science has begun to represent and symbolize this schism.

In the earthly realm, "the activity of our will takes place just as unconsciously as our sleep life."

Even the breath of original life was a product of unconscious clairvoyance. God speaks to people through dreams, and through the countenance of Archangel Michael, while remaining unknown. When clairvoyants pray to God, Michael speaks to them, but only if they are in a state of clairvoyance or meditation similar to sleeping during waking day consciousness. This is because the Michael revelation is, inherently and originally, a revelation of the night. In ancient times, clairvoyants could not be in ordinary consciousness in order to perceive spiritual reality. Luciferic beings were active during waking hours, while divine beings were active at night. Michael was the servant of the ruler of the night (Yave).

In the Anthroposophical view, the head of the human being -- in other words, our waking consciousness -- had, before the Mystery of Golgotha, been more controlled by the Luciferic beings. In consequence, the nighttime consciousness of peace and rest had to stream up and into the head from the rest of the body. Michael was the conduit from heaven who could make this happen. Christ then united himself with human beings through the mystery of Golgotha, providing an additional free will choice for avoiding Luciferic spirits. "Earth evolution first received its real meaning" because the

Divine could, from that point onward, be perceived during daylight hours, thereby creating conscious waking connection with the spiritual world. Not enough time had passed, until the end of the 19th century, since Golgotha for the extent of this true consciousness to be realized; but when 1899 came to pass, the time had come for its full fruition. In an important transition of our time, Michael became the revealer of spiritual light during the day, a pure spirit of day.

Even in pagan times, humankind tried to understand Christianity, knowing instinctively that Luciferic elements must gradually be exposed to other powers in order to break them down. Michael sent his opponents to humankind so that we could receive his reason; then the mystery of Golgotha happened. Michael has participated, since the last third of the 19th century, in a special role with regard to humanity.

With Michael, human beings can access that which is truly spiritual in themselves even if it is opposed by negative powers. Because of who Michael has become, the Arhimanic element must, by necessity, be lifted away. Michael is a spirit of strength, and helps us to avoid both abstract spirituality and excessive bodily materialism. He is able to see the spiritual in matter, and when he is with us, we can do the same, to a certain degree. We have to take the spiritual not just into our mind, but into our whole being -- via Christ impulse, as the interpretation of the Michael impulse.

Michael is the day spirit of Christ. With his influence, which cannot occur unless we ask, human consciousness of all that comprises the outer world becomes spiritualized and sensitive to the divine. We become better able to communicate with loved ones who have passed. Michael is there to remind us to breathe deeply and fully, so that our supersensible abilities can be awakened and the purely physical can begin to contain the spiritual within our supersensible perception.

With the modern conceptualization of Archangel Michael, the human acceptance of nature, as it still exists on earth, has the chance to align itself into harmony with individual personal freedom. We experience an accelerated, heightened sense of consciousness of spiritual life, of the spiritual within all that surrounds us. This prevents caving in to "obscured consciousness" and the infiltration of our psyches by increasingly powerful Arhimanic influences that mislead human populations and pull us down into terrible pain, war and strife.

At the beginning of our earth period, after Archangel Michael's battle with the dragon which resulted in its being cast down onto earth and into human consciousness in the form of intellect, the concurrent downfall of the Luciferic element coincided with the sharp rise of the Arhimanic, which represents destructive forces of will resulting in heavy, hopeless, unaware passivity. In our time, human beings can only regain control of consciousness and wholeness of the self if we unify and align ourselves with Christ in every regard, because Arhimanic forces are always looking for the smallest hole or weakness in our conscious faith as a point of entry.

The help of Archangel Michael therefore becomes very necessary, and can be summoned through a refined perception of breath, air, light and the soul nature inherent in everything around us. In ancient times, human beings possessed a different conceptualization of space and time; they considered the spiritual and natural worlds to be the same, and events could occur simultaneously, without the boundaries our current thought processes contain. The air was filled with soul power, and the earth seemed to breathe in and out along with all of the living creatures upon it. Later, people began to perceive, still through the quality of their breath and the soul quality

135

of the air around them, that the God in nature was the same as the God within themselves. Later still, in the Greek era, a separation between the natural and the spiritual became accepted as the dominant conception. The yogic tradition of India made a beautiful attempt to heal this separation after the fact, and to regain lost unity through the pathway of the breath; but in our time, the air is no longer filled with elemental soul spirit, and we must find a different way of increasing our sensitivity to the spiritual world.

Archangel Michael has a special role in helping us to remember the subtlety of our connection to the external, spiritual worlds, and to remain constantly aware of our soul-based relationship to the earth and the universe. Today, we commonly live with a fragmented, divisive consciousness that contains only a partial conception of all that exists in nature; unfortunately, "reality itself has lost its soul." With the guidance of Michael, we are able to put the soul and the feeling back into the five senses, achieving an elevated comprehension that is at once more sensitive and more spiritually based than before. We must be incredibly strong in this period on earth, and breathe the goodness and purity of nature back into our hearts even as negative forces attempt to veil our awareness and trick us into believing that the poisonous is healthy, that pain is normal, and that limitation, lack and suffering are all we can hope for.

In order to do this, it will be crucial to see and to understand that the soul element, formerly a living presence in the air around us, now exists within light -- not just physical light, but the spiritual light that permeates our souls and the universe. In this way, we will be able to replace the lost air processes of ancient times with a new perception of spiritual light.

This type of Michaelic thinking can be used in meditation, in

136

everyday thought, and in prayers to God, for whom Michael is a chief messenger. Archangel Michael is strongly protective of humankind, and has provided us with the means to allow our soul, body and spirit to work together so that we may become a force for goodness and light far into the future, easily able to access psychic visions and make connections between the worlds.

CHAPTER X

Rebirth

As we have seen, according to universal law, a child must relearn the culture that has advanced since their last death, and must therefore start afresh. Souls wait until the culture they knew in their last incarnation has significantly changed before re-entering physical life.

Before rebirth can occur, we begin the process of contracting until we are as tiny as cells at conception, "quickly or slowly according to our karma," and begin our journey backward, passing once again through each of the planetary spheres. Knowledge is again bestowed upon us in each sphere, this time as we sleep. The embryo comes into being as an expression of the magnificent truth and beauty of the starry realms. We are reborn, "strengthened and refreshed" according to our karma and all of the possibilities it can offer to our lives and to the earth. Our internal spiritual forces have been "built up" by meeting, between death and rebirth, the souls we previously knew on earth. The human embryo now "bears the whole cosmos" within the tiniest of precious forms. We have adapted to the universe.

The constellation under which we are born leaves an imprint upon the soul, which then wants to re-enter life under that same constellation, even at another time and in another part of the world. "We come into the world with wisdom that far exceeds what we are able to acquire later" during physical life.

At birth, the "brain is still soft." During childhood, we undergo an infusion and saturation of earthly knowledge. Before this, though, there exists a "womb of vast spiritual wisdom that precedes the embryonic stage". The further back we psychically travel into the time between death and rebirth, the wiser we see that we are.

In the start of the spirit phase, by contrast, we are old to begin with, then become young as the concerns of earthly life are removed. "At spiritual birth, one becomes young." Between death and rebirth, we expand outward and "take the starry heavens with us". This leaves a moral imprint upon the soul, which is then carried forward into the next life. The "human being feels full responsibility" toward our being; we are responsible to the cosmos because we bear all of it within us. It is our "sacred duty" to bring forth the forces we have gathered from the cosmos, and it is the "greatest sin to allow these forces to lie fallow."

The powers of the etheric body cannot be drawn from the earth during physical life; they can only be found and taken up between death and rebirth. If one takes immorality through the gate of death, however, one is incapable of attracting forces of goodness there. A heightened sense of awareness of the self can lead us to greater spirituality while living in the earthly realm.

Before birth, our souls worked on our ancestors in order to prepare them, and brought together relatives who could provide the "appropriate predispositions" for our lives. A reciprocal understanding is needed between our soul and our ancestors, across time. For example, someone born in the 18th century has already collaborated with ancestors from the 16th century. "We first instill in our ancestors what we later inherit from them."

In Devachan, a pull is exerted upon the soul to live and to become. This occurs between recollection of earlier lives and preparation for future physical lives. This feeling is life expressed in its most heightened state, and represents the polar opposite of death. Beings of the Higher Hierarchies then prepare us for rebirth with regard to chosen time and place of birth, along with the type of body we will receive. The Higher Hierarchies also determine the characteristics of our parents.

In the embryo, "the shape of the head is prefigured astrally" in the last stage before rebirth. Certain other physical characteristics, such as strength, are determined by heredity. In the case of birth defects, Anthroposophy puts forward the possible explanation that the souls were not able to find their ancestors in time to determine appropriate development.

In the higher world, "everything is consciousness." A child who has died may also be read to from anthroposophical text, and is actually less childlike than other souls living in the spiritual world. He or she is "a highly evolved individual", and takes a place of great nobility in the higher worlds before future reincarnation. This is because the early death allowed a great deal of physical life force to remain, transmuted, in the soul; this life force is exceedingly precious, helpful and healing to all souls in all worlds.

In the "gathering-in" for rebirth, the soul is collecting forces "from every part of the zodiac" and focusing upon a center point. The newborn child is sent by the Higher Hierarchies long before conception. It is important to remember that while life can be proven by outer, physical science, it can be equally proven by karma. The soul develops the capability to reach across time to the ancestors, where the seed of our individual life force is planted; we give our qualities and characteristics directly into their safekeeping, and begin preparation for all of the beauty and infinite possibilities of the next life.

A Favor

If you enjoyed this book may I ask a small favor? When you have the time
I would ask that you to go back to Amazon and leave an honest review of
"Reading to the Dead". We are a small boutique publisher and reviews
help us spread the word to the world more effectively. I appreciate your
time and effort. Thank you, Barry J Peterson

Interesting Reads:

The Power of "I AM", a compilation of the Best I AM Quotes
www.ThePowerofIAM.Org
Compiled & Edited by David Allen

How to Create a Power Prayer Group
www.PowerPrayerGroup.Com
Author: Barry J Peterson

Neville Goddard: The Complete Reader
www.NevilleGoddardReader.Com
Author: Neville Goddard

www.ScienceAndHealth1875Edition.Com
Mary Baker Eddy's Original Manuscript

The Sickle (1918)
www.TheSickle.Org William W. Walter

Gnostic Audio Selection:

To access the audio book version of "Reading to the Dead"
please visit www.GnosticAudio.Com and follow the directions
to access your free streaming audio version of this book.
(This is a streaming audio only; audio book is NOT downloadable)

www.AudioEnlightenment.Com
Be sure to check out www.AudioEnlightenmentPress.Com for the latest
publications from the world of Metaphysics

CPSIA information can be obtained
at www.ICGtesting.com
Printed in the USA
FFOW05n1814150414